STRESS
TEFLON

STRESS TEFLON

IT'S GREAT GREAT BEING YOU WHEN STRESS DOESN'T STICK

LUKE MATHERS

WITH MICK ZELJKO

Advantage®

Published by Advantage, Charleston, South Carolina.
Member of Advantage Media Group.

ADVANTAGE is a registered trademark, and the Advantage colophon is a trademark of Advantage Media Group, Inc.

Printed in the United States of America.

10 9 8 7 6 5 4 3 2 1

ISBN: 978-1-59932-801-0
LCCN: 2017932464

Cover design by Katie Biondo.

Advantage Media Group is proud to be a part of the Tree Neutral® program. Tree Neutral offsets the number of trees consumed in the production and printing of this book by taking proactive steps such as planting trees in direct proportion to the number of trees used to print books. To learn more about Tree Neutral, please visit **www.treeneutral.com.**

Advantage Media Group is a publisher of business, self-improvement, and professional development books. We help entrepreneurs, business leaders, and professionals share their Stories, Passion, and Knowledge to help others Learn & Grow. Do you have a manuscript or book idea that you would like us to consider for publishing? Please visit **advantagefamily.com** or call **1.866.775.1696.**

I would like to thank everyone in my tribe who have given me the confidence to write this book. To my beautiful wife, Karen, and daughter, Chloe, thank you for putting up with my ramblings. Thank you to Mick Zeljko. Your ability to make difficult things simple has been crucial to bringing this book to life. Thanks also to Mike Protopsaltis (my Greek ambassador); Greg Young, for making it a book people will want to read; and my editor, Matthew Godbey, who organised my haphazard theories into something real.

It's been fun!

-TABLE OF CONTENTS-

—INTRODUCTION—

'This is my message to you-ou-ou.'

—Bob Marley

What's your relationship with stress? Is stress a huge marlin on the end of your fishing line or are you swimming in open water getting circled by hungry sharks?

'It's really stressful.'

'I'm so stressed.'

'He really stresses me out!'

We hear these comments all the time and it appears more people are in the water with the sharks than pulling in the catch of the day. This book is here to change how you view stress and help you use it to your advantage.

Stress isn't the worst thing in the world. Stress is awesome! Stress helps you get shit done. Stress drives you to take on new challenges. Stress lights a fire in the belly, an essential part of any worthwhile endeavour. If something doesn't have some stress in it, it's not fun— at least not for long. Don't believe me? We can probably all agree that sitting on a beautiful beach all day sipping piña coladas would be great for a few days, maybe even a week. But what about after thirty days? A year? Five years? The prospect of a stress-free life starts to look more boring and depressing as time goes on. After all, what is there to accomplish? What challenge is there to celebrate overcoming?

We hear so much about the downside of stress that I suspect it comes as a surprise to hear what I'm about to tell you: *Stress is not the enemy.*

Was it stressful when Sir Edmund Hillary climbed Everest for the first time? Fuck yes, it was. Was there a lot of stress for Steve Jobs at Apple? Absolutely! Remember how he got sacked by his own board? Did you feel the knot in your stomach during the last minutes of your son's under-tens football final? Of course you did.

Stress is normal. Stress is stimulating. Stress is evolutionary. It keeps us alive. Stress is not the enemy. The problem is the type of stress we have, how long it lasts, and how we've been taught to deal with common stress.

In *Stress Teflon*, we are going to learn why we have stress, how to harness it and use it for good, and how to keep it from sticking to us. To be clear, this book is not about avoiding stress. It's about utilising stress as a tool, a short-term power booster that gives us a kick up the arse and sees us on our way to achieving our potential.

This book isn't about unicorns farting rainbows, either. Certain types of stress are terrible. Childhood leukaemia, tsunamis, losing a loved one, and so much more are all awful types of stressful situations. They suck, they're often unavoidable, and they are proper caveman stressors, which we'll discuss in more detail later. But most types of harmful stress don't come from uncontrollable outside forces. Most of the harmful stress we experience is generated between our own ears. The good news is it's our own fault, and much of today's harmful stress is totally avoidable. This book will teach you why it happens and how to avoid harmful stress while embracing and utilising the stress that is productive.

The ancient Greeks called it *eudemonia* (pronounced u-de-monia for westerners but the Greeks say *ef-dem-on-ea*. Say it a few times, and maybe even throw in a Greek accent!), which translates literally to 'good spirit' but encompasses so much more. By achieving *eudemonia*, you are well on the way to becoming *Stress Teflon*.

Eudemonia: a state of happiness, well-being, and objective flourishing brought on by moral virtue, practical wisdom, and rationality.

The Greeks rock! They may not be able to run an economy, and feta cheese tastes a bit like socks, but the Greeks have had some pretty smart dudes.

I love the concept of *eudemonia*: objective flourishing. How could you not want to objectively flourish? To me, *eudemonia* is about making *your* world a better place. That doesn't mean Louis Vuitton, McMansions, and Ferraris. It means living a life of meaning, of helping others, of contributing to your tribe, and of being happy in your own skin. How much of the bad stress in your life would disappear if you believed in yourself? How much stress is generated by self-doubt? If you achieve *eudemonia*, this bad stress, generated from self-doubt, disappears.

So often we hear people say, 'If only I had _____, then I would be happy.' This way of thinking has it backward. Happiness is a choice, not a destination. Searching for happiness is a bit like an orgasm—the harder you look for it, the less likely you are to find it. Becoming *Stress Teflon* will make it easier for you to choose happiness. *Eudemonia* will be your default position.

Losing your job, failing exams, or breaking bones are all temporary blips in a life of eighty-plus years. As my mother-in-law would put it, they are splinters in your bum as you slide down the bannister of life. These things are stressful in the short term, absolutely. But if you are *Stress Teflon*, you have a belief in yourself that will ensure you overcome the blips. The pride generated from overcoming adversity will become the foundations of self-belief and *eudemonia*.

If you are going to objectively flourish, you need to believe in yourself. And when you have that genuine belief, all of the stress associated with self-doubt will disappear. Imagine your default position is that it's great being you. Would you care if your arse looks big in those jeans? Would you care if your car was not the latest model, and would you be stressed about what John from accounting thinks of you? No, you would not give these thoughts any oxygen. If you had *eudemonia*, you would know that you are a good person and if John from accounting doesn't like you, that would be John's problem, not yours.

The Stanford researcher and stress expert Kelly McGonigal has, for years, studied the effects of stress on health. Together with her colleagues, she concluded that chasing meaning is more important than avoiding stress.[1] In other words, stress is not the enemy; the belief that stress is the enemy is the enemy.

Several years ago Professor McGonigal began to wonder about the effects of stress. She had believed, like most of us, that stress was harmful to our health—so harmful, in fact, that the mere existence of stress in our lives would surely kill us and therefore should be avoided at all costs. But when a team of researchers at the University of Wisconsin released a study on the perception of stress in 2012, all that changed for McGonigal.[2]

---

1   "How to make stress your friend," TED, June 2013, https://www.ted.com/talks/kelly_mcgonigal_how_to_make_stress_your_friend.

2   A. Keller, K. Litzelman, L. E. Wisk, T. Maddox, E. R. Cheng, P. D. Creswell, and W. P. Witt, 'Does the perception that stress affects health matter? The association with health and mortality', *Health Psychology* 31 (5): 677–684, http://www.ncbi.nlm.nih.gov/pubmed/22201278.

The researchers looked at data from a 1998 US National Health Interview Survey and compared their findings to the US National Death Index mortality data through 2006. The data showed that 33.7 per cent of nearly 186 million US adults perceived that stress affected their health a lot or to some extent. If you're like me, then the most surprising thing about that finding is that *only* 33.7 per cent thought stress affected their physical health.

But what's more surprising is that when correlating the amount of stress and the perception that stress affects health, those who reported a lot of stress and that stress impacted their health a lot had a 43 per cent *increased* risk of premature death. As McGonigal now argues, the research hints at the idea that the belief that stress is harmful is actually more harmful than the stress itself. If you believe stress helps, it does. If you believe stress is harmful to your health, it is. How you choose to view stress is the difference. It is your choice and this book will give you the knowledge and tools to make stress your friend.

Public speaking is one of just about everyone's top three stressful experiences. Just before walking up to the podium, your heart will be pounding, you may be a little fidgety, and there will be a few butterflies in the pit of your stomach. That's stress! Now imagine lining up to go on the latest vertical-drop, triple-loop, death-defying rollercoaster. The feeling is almost identical (with the possible addition of sphincter cramp). Both fire up the same responses in our bodies, one we stress about for days beforehand and one we do for fun. Biologically, though, they are the same. The difference is how long the stress lasts and where it is generated. Does this same biological stress response give you a heart attack and an ulcer, or does it make for a great story you tell your friends about later? The choice is yours.

This book will help you identify the forks in the stress road and help you take the road that uses stress to achieve great things rather than sending you to the cardiac ward. Being self-aware and catching yourself at the fork in the stress road are the keys to making sure you use stress in a positive way.

To understand why we have stress and how to use it to our advantage, we are going to wander back ten thousand years. There I'll introduce you to our hero, Cronk, and look at life before agriculture, civilization, and iPhones. We will look at how our brains tick, why we live in groups (or tribes), what makes us thrive, and what drives us to find purpose in our lives.

Stress is not the big, bad enemy it's made out to be. Once you understand a bit more about how we have evolved, it will be clear why we behave the way we do.

Quality living is about finding your purpose, choosing happiness, and learning to chase meaning rather than avoiding stress. So let's choose a new direction in the stress road together. Let's choose the stress road that gets shit done, the road that fires us up to do good things for ourselves and the people we love. This road is where you feel proud of yourself, and that pride will enable you to climb any mountain and do great things. It may be stressful, but embrace it. Stress is here to stay and it's here to help.

SECTION I

UNDERSTANDING HOW WE TICK AND HOW WE GOT TO HERE

— CHAPTER 1 —

GOODBYE, CRONK: A BRIEF HISTORY OF PRIMAL HUMANS

'Study the past if you would define the future.'

—Confucius

The tribe was nearly silent as they stood, shoulder to shoulder, huddled in a large circle around the shallow grave. It was winter, a time when the cold seemed to make death even more common than usual. Most wiped tears from their eyes, and a quiet sniffling sometimes rose from the shivering mass. He was dead now, the brave leader they had loved and relied upon for so many winters.

In the pit, Cronk's body lay wrapped tightly in large leaves, and two tiger fangs rested on his chest. Above them, positioned atop a granite boulder jutting high and flat from the earth, their new elder, Brac, began to speak.

Today we have full stomachs and heavy hearts. The summer has been good to us. We have had warm months and the hunting and fruit have been plentiful. The gods have smiled on us for many days, but today they have made us sad. The gods have decided that they need Cronk more than we do, and we must trust in the wisdom of the gods.

Tears made clear lines down his cheeks as he spoke, but Brac made no effort to wipe them away. He had just watched his mentor and oldest friend die. Now Brac only wanted the tribe—young and old—to know what an amazing man Cronk was, how important he had been to them all.

Cronk has seen many summers and has been a friend, father, or teacher to everyone here. When we were small, all Cronk and I wanted to do was hunt. We would make spears so small that they could only kill birds. He was always able to get closer to the birds and never missed with the spear. Spears were always sharp, and he would practice by throwing them at the high fruit in the trees.

He learnt to track from his father, and he could follow every kind of creature for many days. As a young hunter, he was strong and fast, always sensing where to attack and when to defend. Even after a long day of tracking, he could creep up on an animal and run with it long enough to get his deadly spear to hit the mark.

He loved coming home after a successful hunt, too. He could single-handedly carry a boar for a whole day, and no one stood taller than a young Cronk when he dropped the carcass in the camp.

There was a real joy in Brac's voice as he talked about his friend. Something in his face and body, too, spoke louder than his words, the way he tightened and eased in rhythm with his memories of Cronk. He continued:

Everyone loved to be with Cronk and hear him tell of his hunting adventures. No one who was there will ever forget when our group came face to face with the lone tiger. Cronk stood between us and the fierce animal. As the giant tiger charged, he held his ground, threw his spear with all his might, and lanced the animal in the heart as it bounded forward. That night we feasted on roasted tiger and retold the story over and over again. The magnitude of Cronk's bravery was not lost on anyone. He wore his tiger skin with great pride, and its two giant teeth were always at his side.

Brac paused for a moment, smiling to himself as he remembered a folk tale he and Cronk had learned when they were kids. He went on:

There are so many other stories we should know, too, like the one about the four oxen that stood tail to tail so that when any lion came near, it would always be met by horns. The oxen grew big and strong until arguments split the four apart. Once they no longer stood tail to tail, the lions killed them one by one. Stories like this are what made Cronk our leader. He made us realise that everyone is important and that by doing our part and working together, we will all have full stomachs and a safe life.

Everyone could feel the gratitude in Brac's voice as he talked about his old friend, and the quiet sobs began to soften, the sullen faces in the crowd brightening now with hope and pride. He spoke his last words:

In more recent times, Cronk had found it difficult to keep up with the young hunters. His bones were growing old and weary. He spent many days helping the younger ones discover their skills, encouraging them to be brave and telling stories of the great hunts of his youth. All the young hunters wanted to grow up and make Cronk proud of them. When it was time for them to become men, it was Cronk who led them out and told them his stories.

Tomorrow, we will leave this place, but it will always hold a special place in our hearts as we remember Cronk and give thanks for the lessons he has taught us—lessons of skill, bravery, teamwork, love, and caring. You will be missed, my friend.

* * *

If we were writing your eulogy right now, did you kill a 'tiger,' something that frightened you immensely? Did you look after the kids as you got older? Would you pass away with the same reverence that Cronk did? Has your life touched people like his life did? We've come a long way since the days when a scene like Cronk's funeral might have taken place, but are we really that much different from the prehistoric versions of our present-day selves?

Now, I know what you're thinking. How do you know so much about this Cronk bloke? Truth is Cronk didn't write much stuff down, but a century or so of genetics and anthropology research now suggests we are much more like the Cronks of our past than we think we are. Our species has been evolving for hundreds of thousands, perhaps even millions, of years. During that time we have become the most well-adapted and influential species in Earth's history—at least we like to think so.

We've learned to thrive as a communal species rather than just survive in the wild like our more primitive ancestors. We might have more or less started out hunkered in caves and holes for protection, armed with little more than sticks and stones, but we managed to build massive cities and weapons capable of destroying ourselves and just about everything else, too. Our collective accomplishments and foresight are vital to the forward progress that our survival demands. But to better understand our body, our brain, and our tribe, it pays to look backwards from time to time. We will learn a lot about modern life from Cronk.

Whether you agree or disagree or even understand the intricate theories behind human evolution isn't all that important. But there is an intersection of science, medicine, history, and sociology that will help us get a handle on why we do what we do. The modern world is rapidly changing. Technology has made us more connected than ever before, and the stress of staying competitive and happy in a time when productivity is more likely to be measured on a digital spectrum than a human one is, at times, overwhelming. But by understanding our primal traits, we can get better at handling stress, modernizing our instincts, and thus strengthening every facet of our lives from health to attitude to career to relationships.

If you thought this was supposed to be a book for everyday people but find yourself feeling you stepped into the wrong class, don't worry. You're in the right place. This isn't a palaeontology thesis by any means, and if it were, we would all be in trouble. I'm certainly not the go-to expert for the latest news on fossil digs, genome discoveries, and the like. We'll leave that to people much smarter than I am.

If you hadn't figured it out already, I'm just a regular guy with a regular life, a small-business owner, husband, and father. I've watched some people thrive in times of stress, and I've seen others be debilitated by it. But when I found myself twenty-five years into my chosen career, I stopped, had a look around, and got curious. Why do some people handle everything that's thrown at them and others don't? I've since spent the last several years researching human instincts and behaviour to try to understand why.

At our most primal, every living person has the same basic needs: shelter, food, and water (and maybe sex, too, to ensure the species survives). That's it. Just *three or four* things! Sounds easy, right? But of course it's not really that simple. Survival was a little more complicated for Cronk and his tribe than a cave, a hunk of meat, and a bit of water all those thousands of years ago, and it's certainly more complicated for us today. Our safety from predators and disease, our innate need to feel we contribute and are part of a tribe, our biological instinct to reproduce—they are all equally important to us both then and now, not only for our survival but to be able to thrive once we do.

Driving that desire to thrive is the instinctual fear we all have of our own extinction. As a result, we focus on the negatives of our experiences more than the positives to ensure that we learn and advance accordingly. We want to avoid repeating painful experiences, meaning we are always searching for easier ways to exist.

Finding a mate and gaining acceptance and respect in our tribe depend, in part, on how we look and carry ourselves. Of course, none of our aesthetics will matter if a disease is going to kill us before we even get a chance to flaunt them in the first place. So while our environment may change over time, as we move from, say, the jungle to the singles bar or the boardroom, our primal instincts remain the same: find shelter, find water, find food, find a mate, protect your tribe, and then you will have done what you are here to do.

But as our environment grows more civil, more convenient, and more elaborate, it also becomes more difficult for our primal instincts to navigate. When that happens, the confusion between instinct and invention, natural and unnatural, causes a lot of chronic stress in our lives, much of that stress being generated in our own heads.

For Cronk, danger was readily apparent. Even though his survival required constant alertness and a quick, well-executed reaction, the threat was at least fairly easy to spot. After all, you can mistake a tree for a lion a hundred times and you are okay. Mistake a lion for a tree, however, and you are no longer contributing to evolution. *This is why we tend to focus more on the negatives.*

But for us, the lion is often either something of our mind's own making or it's something that's much more subtle than an actual lion, a threat or fear buried beneath thousands of years of social evolution. The only way to slay the lion now is to understand who we were then, back when our primal ways determined our very survival.

You can begin by asking three simple questions when you're faced with a threat or problem:

- What am I thinking?

- Why am I thinking it?

- Is it helping?

Think of these questions as a three-part *eudemonia* quiz for the rational decision-making process we'll explore in the coming chapters

– CHAPTER 2 –

MODERN-DAY TIGERS

*'Walking with a friend in the dark is better
than walking alone in the light.'*

—Helen Keller

The story of Cronk slaying the tiger is a fantastic way to look at
stress in all its life-saving glory. But since there are very few tigers
wandering around suburbia in the twenty-first century, I want to
share with you a more modern story about tigers of a different kind.

It was a warm November morning in Queensland, a common
forecast for Australia's Sunshine State. I was driving my daughter,
Chloe, to school when I got a phone call from one of my best friends,
Shaun 'Shakey' Stephens. After the usual pleasantries and a quick
warning that we were on loudspeaker, Shaun's tone of voice changed.
'Mate, I've got some bad news', he said. Shakey, it should be noted,
isn't just a good mate; he's also my accountant. That combination will
present new depths of fear when the simple phrase 'I've got bad news'
is uttered, even deeper anxieties when your daughter is listening on
an otherwise routine morning drive. I felt my heart creeping into my
throat. Over the previous six months, we'd had to deal with a lot of
issues surrounding the selling of one of my businesses, and I knew
this had the potential to be much worse news than Shaun cancelling

dinner plans. I swallowed hard and could immediately feel my heart starting to race as I blurted out the first thing that came to mind.

'For fuck's sake, Shakey, I've paid enough fucking *tax*!' I bellowed, my warnings about speakerphones and thirteen-year-old daughters now a distant memory. 'I'm not paying any more fucking tax!'

'Hold on, big fella', Shaun said calmly. 'It's not always about you.' His last words shook me. He was right. I had assumed that his news was somehow all about me. I felt like a complete asshole, and I could almost feel myself flushed with embarrassment as Shaun went on to tell me about a recent troubling development with another friend of ours, Craig, or Rags as everyone affectionately calls him. In fact, I had known Rags for five years before I'd ever heard anyone refer to him by his actual name. Rags, as it turned out, had just been diagnosed with a brain tumour. The details of the tumour were still a bit sketchy, but he had lost his sense of smell and had been getting severe headaches. My tax issues all forgotten, I felt a much different tightening in my stomach and a lump in my throat.

I didn't have a lot of experience with close friends getting life-threatening illnesses, so my immediate response was to investigate what I could do to help. There was a sense of helplessness that came over me after Shaun and I hung up. I had recently been doing a lot of research on brain biology and the loss-of-smell symptom really concerned me. The olfactory bulb (the part of the brain responsible for smell) lies deep in the limbic system of the human brain, the old-school part of our minds. That is not a good place to go digging around with brain surgery. The tightness in my stomach remained as I dropped Chloe at school and rather unconvincingly reassured her that Rags would be okay.

When we talk about caveman worries, this is one of them. This is life and death, and the thought of losing a good friend before the age of fifty was not a comfortable one. It was stressful for us, imagining how Ragsy must be feeling. Whether we know it or not, we all crave a kind of stability, or homeostasis, within our minds and bodies. An instinctual need for stability, health, and well-being rules most of our thoughts and actions on a daily basis. As I drove out of the school that day, I was a long way from homeostasis and not at all comfortable about it.

Tightness in the stomach and a lump in the throat are both stress responses associated with our flight-or-fight reflex, a survival instinct controlled by the older parts of our brains. The fact that we are not in direct danger from, say, a tiger attack does not change this reflex's release of stress hormones. Shaun's news had triggered the same response in me. So, with stress hormones pumping through my system, I felt tense and jittery. I needed to get some form of control over the situation to decrease my discomfort.

It may sound like cheap advice, but *deep breathing* is one of the best ways to take control of your fear response when faced with a threat, whether it's real or perceived. You can't take long, slow, deep breaths while running away from a tiger. I was fortunate and remembered that tactic just in time. Several deep breaths later, my heart rate began to slow and I could think straight again, as my brain moved its focus away from panic and on to helping my friend.

None of my friends know more about brains than Mick Zeljko does. He's not a doctor, but he is doing his PhD in cognitive neuroscience and has a great ability to explain complex things really simply. I got straight on the phone with him and explained Ragsy's predicament. Sharing my concern about the smell symptoms, Mick went into research mode. Within twenty minutes, we had come up with the most likely cause: a meningioma. Meningioma are tumours that grow from the meninges, or the fluid-filled sac that surrounds our brain. They can grow quite large before eliciting any symptoms and are usually not fatal. If you're going to have a brain tumour, this is the one you want. Because they are on the outside of the brain, meningioma are generally quite treatable with surgery and rarely return, which meant that the prognosis for Ragsy was very good.

The next day, we got a phone call from Ragsy, confirming Mick's suggested diagnosis. Surgery was booked for that day and the offending tumour was removed.

When I walked into Ragsy's hospital room a few days later, I found the sense of relief was palpable. Surrounded by family and friends, he sat up in bed while everyone else in the room talked about how scared they were at the prospect of losing a friend, a dad, a husband, a son, a brother, and so on. It's an interesting choice of word, 'scared.' No one else was in danger, and no one else had a big bald patch and scar on the back of the head like Ragsy did, but we were all scared. The prospect of losing a loved one triggered the same response as being in danger ourselves.

All the visitors bought gifts, magazines, or books, not because they had to but because everyone wanted to do something to *help*. A couple of sporting magazines or some Ferrero Roches were the closest we could get to helping Ragsy slay his tiger.

When I visited Ragsy a few days later, on a quiet Wednesday, it was great for just the two of us to have a chat. Without the hordes of well-wishers, he opened up about how scared he was at the prospect of a life cut short. It wasn't the thought of dying that scared him, though. 'Only the good die young', he joked. It was the thought of how his wife, Jocelyn, and his two teenage kids, Tyson and Kianna, would have handled life without him. 'It's good to be needed, and it's nice to be loved. I just have to hang around to be there for them now. That's what I care about.'

Five months later, we celebrated Ragsy's fiftieth. We had nearly lost him at forty-nine, so the joy in the air had an extra element to it. The tribe was intact, and all were happier for it.

– C H A P T E R 3 –

OLD BRAIN VERSUS NEW BRAIN

*'Look deep into nature and you will
understand everything better.'*

—Albert Einstein

Some years ago, when my family and I were vacationing in Hawaii, I found myself stopped at an intersection while driving around the North Shore, a relatively rural region of the Pacific island state. The place is famous for its great surfing locations—and infamous for the overzealous locals dedicated to protecting them from tourists. In the eyes of the residents there, the island is *their* island and everyone else is something of an intruder. Locals are known to be territorial, and a kind of pissing contest is easy to spark for any number of unwritten infractions. I wasn't thinking about that fact when the driver behind me began aggressively blowing his horn as we waited for the traffic to clear an intersection. I couldn't go anywhere, and as any good Australian would know, if someone is being an idiot, you are obliged to tell them to pull their head in. My reaction to the road-raging goose behind me was to flip him the bird and proceed on my way without giving it a thought.

A little ways down the road, however, I checked my rearview mirror and the driver behind me was going off his chops. For the next few miles afterward, the driver, now totally enraged, sped within inches of our rented convertible while appearing to have a spasm and shouting every curse word imaginable at me. When we pulled into Polynesian World, the big empty car park made us feel like the Griswolds from *National Lampoon's Vacation* (we were an hour early). I parked the convertible and the crazy man followed us and parked a few spots away. He hopped out of his truck, drew a machete—a machete!—from under the bench seat his three small children were sitting on, and came charging toward our car. I froze and kept myself calm by repeating, 'He's just scaring the tourist . . . he's just scaring the tourist . . .' I managed to keep calm and apologize for my offending finger ('I hate it when it does that . . .' *Top Gun*, anyone?). When he grabbed the driver's seat behind my shoulder, seemingly intent on teeing off on my head, my wife said firmly, 'Take your hands off my husband.' With that, the man looked at my wife and then at my daughter in the backseat and backed off. He calmed a bit and suddenly looked at me as a dad and a husband. He saw me as a person, not just some arsehole tourist with an uncontrollable middle finger. In his view, I was being disrespectful. Not only that, but he also said I was 'setting a bad example' for my child. He was right. Flipping the bird is a bad example for my daughter. I'm not sure he was the best one to be giving parenting advice, as his three kids had front row seats to his tantrum and their eyes were fixed on him as he went at the tourist with the machete. But, then again, this wasn't my environment and I wasn't a member of his tribe. We had different rules.

Nonetheless, there was something else happening between us, despite our differences in rationale and temperament. The angry driver, at the time of his outburst, was being completely controlled by a different brain from the one controlling him before my wife made him aware that he was about to attack a husband and father. She made him realise his reaction was over the top and he saw reason.

When you talk about stress, having a rampant, territorial Hawaiian come at you with a machete is up there on the list of stressful situations. In this chapter, we are going to have a look at the brain and how it has evolved to handle stress to help us determine where the stress originated.

Millions of years of evolution have seen the human brain develop like an onion: in layers. There are a bunch of different areas of the brain

that I'm not going to bore you with. Scientific jargon—like dorsal anterior cingulate, hippocampus, amygdala, and cerebellum—isn't necessary for our purposes, but there is a brain box included here if you are interested. I am not a neurobiologist; I am a simple bloke, and for the purpose of this book, we are going to split the brain into two parts, the Old Brain and the New Brain.

The Old Brain is directly linked to the spinal cord and is our reactive part of the brain. The Old Brain is essentially where reflex responses arise, where repetitive routines are stored and primal attributes are remembered. It's sometimes called the reptilian brain or the old mammalian brain and is the most basic mechanism left over from our primitive ancestors.

Your Old Brain is great at keeping you alive. Superbly evolved, it quickly and automatically detects threats in the environment and then triggers a cascade of nerve impulses and brain chemicals that enable you to do something about it. Before you even know it, you've jumped five feet, turned, and run away, or, like Cronk, you've expertly speared the tiger in the heart. The problem, though, is that in becoming so optimised at keeping you alive, the Old Brain has made a few trade-offs.

BRAIN BOX: BRAIN BASICS

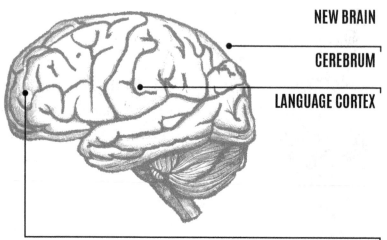

NEW BRAIN

CEREBRUM

LANGUAGE CORTEX

PREFRONTAL CORTEX

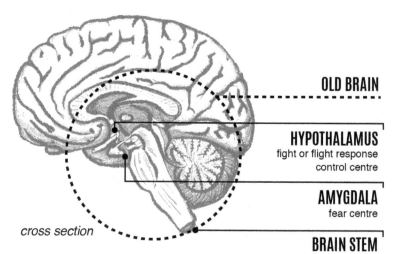

OLD BRAIN

HYPOTHALAMUS
fight or flight response
control centre

AMYGDALA
fear centre

cross section

BRAIN STEM
two-way brain-body connection

First, it is negatively biased. It will focus on the negative life-threatening possibilities before it sees the positive options. This means that you are much more likely to perceive something non-threatening as threatening rather than the reverse. Secondly, your Old Brain's detection system isn't very nuanced, so it isn't exactly grading threats on any type of scale. Things are seen in black and white. Situations you face are classified as either threatening or not threatening without any 'mildly threatening' setting in between. Finally, your Old Brain's response system is similarly not very nuanced. The *fight-or-flight* response is either on (if there's a threat) or off (if there is not). The first makes sense since, in an uncertain world, you're better off jumping out of the way of a snake than not jumping out of the way of a snake. It makes sense as speed-accuracy trade-offs. Don't waste precious time working out how bad a situation is or how fully to respond. If it's bad, go and go hard.

The Old Brain has no ability to use language. When you have a gut feeling about something, it has nothing to do with your digestive system. It is all Old Brain. Gut feeling is the way we describe it because, without words, we can't explain why we feel how we do. We just feel it. The Old Brain looks at the world as good or bad and reacts accordingly. We have had the Old Brain longer than we have had language, so the Old Brain is really good at reading people's body language but not so good at understanding their words. Ever met someone and thought he *felt* dodgy? That is your Old Brain reacting to the subtle cues that person is giving off in the way he holds himself. Intuitive people are very good at listening and interpreting what the Old Brain *feels*. My wife has an amazing bullshit radar. She can easily spot someone whose words and body language don't correlate. She doesn't know why she gets these feelings, but

I have learnt in our twenty-plus years together to listen to her gut feelings. Her Old Brain is usually a pretty good judge.

Most animals live their entire lives ruled by the Old Brain (it's all they have). It's why your placid, friendly dog might viciously snap at you should you get too close when he's eating. The great thing about being human, though, is that we have this amazing *New Brain* sitting on top of the Old Brain that is able to monitor what's going on and modulate our responses accordingly. It's called cognitive control and it enables us to assess the situation, realise that we're not about to die, formulate a plan to deal with the situation, and calm things down. The New Brain is the supervisor! It's slow, but it's smart, nuanced, and powerful. The New Brain can plan, understand shades of grey, and has evolved in a complex social environment to protect you from the Old Brain. As the supervisor, the New Brain should be checking to see if interpretations and responses are reasonable and appropriate.

That doesn't mean that the New Brain is more important or better than the Old Brain. Both are essential to our survival, just in different ways. We need the Old Brain for emotions and survival instincts, and we need the New Brain to mediate what to use from the Old Brain and when.

Our Hawaiian encounter was the result of the Old Brain taking over the enraged driver's New Brain. He had perceived a threat, and his Old Brain had taken control to neutralize that threat. Lucky for me, his New Brain regained control just in time to save me from a close encounter with a machete.

This concept of the two parts of the brain staying connected is the key to understanding stress. The interaction between your Old and New Brain is crucial to both understanding stress and how to get better at dealing with it and using it to your advantage.

Just like my initial reaction to my accountant friend telling me he had bad news, the Old Brain has a tendency to take over in our modern world when it isn't beneficial. It gets confused and reverts to its most primal state. In both situations, a few breaths and some cooler heads saved the day. Once the Old Brain calms, the New Brain is able to say, 'It's okay. We're fine. Why don't you let me take this one?' With that, rational decision making takes over, shirt collars are released, and everyone carries on to make smarter choices. Had my Hawaiian mate had a true threat, the Old Brain would have stayed in command, instincts would have gone full throttle, and someone would have gotten bloodied—most likely me.

THE RATIONALE OF REACTIONS

I'm a city boy, but my wife and I decided to explore some of the remote areas of Tasmania, a little island off the bottom coast of Australia. We had heard that a ten-mile hike up a well-worn trail would take us to a beautiful waterfall called Montezuma Falls, so we drove out to a remote car park and prepared for our day's adventure. I slipped my brand-new hiking boots on, after I'd used a box's worth of Band-Aids on my heels and toes to keep my feet from looking like bubble wrap by the end of the day. I applied sunblock on my face, threw a few water bottles in my backpack and headed into the wild. I felt like Steve Irwin, confident and ready for anything—or so I thought.

It turns out that the trail was actually a defunct railway track. As we started walking along the old tracks, I found it impossible not to think of the movie *Stand by Me*. Before long, Karen and I were whistling and singing songs and balancing ourselves on this railway track like a couple of kids out to explore some alluring mystery.

About two hundred yards down the railway track, still within eyesight of the car, I heard a scream and felt myself jump backwards. The scream was my own. I mean this was a blood-curdling, high-pitched squeal that surprised even me. As if that wasn't embarrassing enough, I had jumped backwards without even knowing it and grabbed my wife, Karen, pulling her backwards with me. I had no idea why. All I heard was a really girly scream (mine), and then I looked down to see a large brown snake on the path right in front of me.

This particular snake is one of the five most dangerous snakes in the world, and there it was sitting right in our path. My heart started beating a hundred miles an hour, and I struggled to get enough air. Once I was clear from the danger, I could only stare at the snake. It took me another few minutes to get my breathing and heart rate under control and actually calm down. My Old Brain had reacted instantly to deal with a threat I wasn't even totally aware of yet. It had sent me flying back into protective mode long before I had any idea that there was a deadly snake in front of me, and I might just be alive today because of it.

In certain situations, your Old Brain is a really good thing and should be allowed to act on its own. But once the Old Brain identifies and reacts to an immediate threat, you need to allow your New Brain to assess the situation and find a proper solution. In my case, the Old Brain's immediate response was, 'Oh! This is bad. The car is right there . . . let's go!' But once the New Brain kicked in, I had more rational thoughts. 'Well, I'm safe at this distance. The snake is just warming itself in the open sunlight and isn't interested in us. I'm sure this whole place isn't covered with brown snakes. Let's just stay vigilant and keep going instead.' I had reconnected my two brains and thought it through.

I was still on edge, as my stress response had triggered a rush of adrenaline in my body, but I was calm enough to make the decision to forge ahead. Karen and I walked around the tanning snake and went on to see the beautiful falls. We had a lovely walk and really enjoyed our time walking that old railway track in Tasmania, snakes and all, thanks to our New Brains being strong enough to stay linked or integrated with our reactive Old Brains.

This interaction between the Old Brain and the New Brain is constantly at play. These regions talk to one another endlessly, as we shop for groceries, drive the car, work, and communicate. The better each of our regions is at deciding who's in charge and when, the closer we are to achieving what's known as vertical integration. Vertical integration, for our purposes, is really just a functional working relationship between the Old Brain and New Brain.

The 1983 movie *Trading Places*, with Dan Aykroyd and Eddie Murphy, provides us with a great illustration of vertical integration at work. The movie tells the story of a born-and-bred, upper-class commodities broker, Louis Winthorpe III (Aykroyd), switching lives with a destitute street hustler, Billy Ray Valentine (Murphy), the result of a slightly sadistic social experiment carried out by two billionaire brothers with opposing views on the ongoing nature versus nurture debate.

When we meet the main characters, they're both comfortable in their respective worlds on opposite ends of the social hierarchy spectrum. Winthorpe enjoys his days playing racquetball at the club, managing his stable stocks, and wining and dining at his luxurious mansion with his fiancé. Valentine, on the other hand, spends his days trying to con strangers for change and navigating his way around the very real line between legal and illegal. Both handle the stress in their lives with ease.

But after the meddling brothers enact their plan to frame Winthorpe for fraud and hire Valentine to take his place, the pair's lives are quickly turned upside down. All of a sudden, everything they used to know and be able to depend on is gone, for better and for worse. Both Winthorpe and Valentine are thrown for a loop, finding themselves overwhelmed by stress and confusion over whom and what to trust and whom and what to avoid. By integrating their Old and New Brains, the boys find solutions and manage to use the stressful situation as an advantage.

In a familiar, safe environment, we get lazy. Our brains are well accustomed to our surrounding conditions, so deciphering a threat and a non-threat occurs very quickly, often subconsciously. In other words, we let our guard down and our New Brain (the supervisor) gets lazy. But like Winthorpe and Valentine after they'd been flung into new lives, intense stress surfaces when our brain doesn't understand new environments. Everything seems like a threat, and our Old Brain takes control to protect us. It's *fight-or-flight* time all the time. That type of stress is not good for long periods. It makes us defensive, as if we were fighting for survival. The New Brain goes offline, focusing us on finding problems, blocking our rational New Brain from finding solutions. In short, constant toxic stress makes us defensive and dumb!

HOW WE ARE WIRED

When we look at how the brain works, we have a look at neural pathways and how our brains are wired. There are about a hundred billion neurons in the average human brain and each one is connected to thousands of others, creating literally trillions of neural pathways. Some of these pathways are short, some are long, some are weak, and some are strong and it is the activity in these pathways, the neurons talking to each other, that creates all your thoughts, behaviours, and actions. I like to think of neural pathways as being like paths in a sand dune. Your natural way of walking to the beach is on the most well-worn path. It is possible to walk over the other parts of the dune, but it's more difficult. Humans are a bit like electricity and water. We will take the path of least resistance.

Habits are our brains sticking to well-worn paths. We think a certain way, because we've always thought a certain way. When people say things like 'I've always had a bad temper', they are saying that the pathways between Old and New Brains aren't very well worn. The integration between Old and New Brains isn't a habit for them. The good thing is you can make new paths in the sand dune. You just have to consciously walk in a different direction and make new paths. It takes more effort but it is possible. You have to decide to keep your two brains integrated and have a better way of working out who's in charge for a given circumstance. You have to make this a habit. The great thing about sand dunes (and neural pathways) is that every time you make yourself take that new, better path, it becomes a little more worn, until one day soon that new path is the most well-worn path and you don't even realise that you're taking it. Don't look now, but you have created a new habit.

So it's not so much *what* you think—it's *how* you think that matters. By integrating the Old Brain and New Brain, smoothing out the communication between the regions, you can process true threats more accurately and make better decisions about how to react to them, which means that with good vertical integration between Old Brain and New Brain, you won't be ready to behead a tourist in front of his family over a hand gesture, and you'll avoid deadly snakes—although doing it without squealing like a little girl, and stumbling, would be nice, too.

WHERE DOES THE STRESS COME FROM?

Now that we understand the concepts of New Brain and Old Brain, I want to look at where stress comes from. In the snake story, the stress came from our external environment, the Old Brain dealt with it quickly and saved the day. This type of stress is short-term, in and out, and is a life-saving reaction to the environment. Cronk had heaps of this type of stress, and evolution ensured that we are really good at dealing with it.

Our New Brain is where our rational thinking comes from and is supposed to help. But, if we have this amazing New Brain that can talk us down off the ledge, *why* do we persist in reacting to manageable modern stressors as if they were a life-threatening tiger coming at us? The problem isn't a failure to stop your Old Brain from reacting (you can't), nor is it a problem of not engaging your New Brain (all you've been doing is thinking about this). The problem is that your New Brain is monitoring the wrong thing. Rather than assessing the actual external situation and determining you're not about to die and can handle this, your New Brain is assessing your internal feelings (the *fight-or-flight* response already initiated by the much faster, automatic Old Brain) and determining that your heart's racing; you have a pit in your stomach; you're terrified—*Holy crap! This must be bad!* Your New Brain's been hijacked by the Old Brain's initial response, so instead of calming things down, it tells the Old Brain to keep going. The *fight-or-flight* response continues, and because the New Brain assesses the reaction as bad, it tells the Old Brain to keep going until your brain is on an out-of-control feedback loop. Before you know it, a manageable situation leads to over-reaction and then to rumination, turning beneficial acute stress into harmful chronic stress and crippling anxiety or a full-blown panic attack.

Where did the stress come from with machete man in Hawaii? My uncontrolled middle finger was hardly a threat to life and limb, yet his Old Brain went into overdrive, started a fight response, and rage ensued. This type of stress starts in the New Brain, which fires up the Old Brain. There is a problem with this type of stress: it lacks per-spective. If the stress originates in the New Brain (*Fuck that tourist!*) and not as a result of a true external threat, the stress can occur at any time for any reason. The New Brain fires up the stress response in the Old Brain, and the New Brain then rationalises the physical reactions from the Old Brain and you end up with a feedback loop of stress.

For Cronk, there was an external threat or there wasn't. He either dealt with the situation or got mauled to death. The threat was external and short-lived. This is how we have evolved. We are really good at this type of stress. An antelope will run like the wind to escape a lion. Once safe though, the antelope will casually go back to chowing down grass as if everything were okay. Antelopes don't have a New Brain.

HAWAIIAN STRESS FEEDBACK LOOP

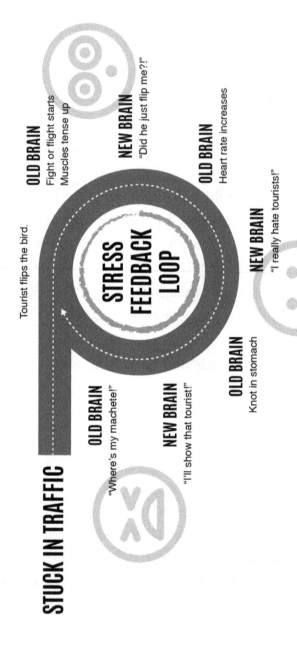

STUCK IN TRAFFIC

Tourist flips the bird.

OLD BRAIN
Fight or flight starts
Muscles tense up

NEW BRAIN
"Did he just flip me?!"

OLD BRAIN
Heart rate increases

NEW BRAIN
"I really hate tourists!"

OLD BRAIN
Knot in stomach

NEW BRAIN
"I'll show that tourist!"

OLD BRAIN
"Where's my machete!"

STRESS FEEDBACK LOOP

The problem is most modern stressors are different. They are New-Brain generated, and as such, they are always there whenever you think of a what-if scenario: What if I can't pay the rent? What if I fail this exam? What if I lose my job? This is where anxiety comes from. Anxiety is the New Brain creating thoughts that generate Old-Brain stress responses and causes thoughts to ruminate between your two brains. My wife, Karen, calls this 'renting a room in your head for free.' As we said, stressors can come from your external environment or they can come from your New Brain thinking of something stressful. Either way, the Old Brain will fire up a physical and emotional response. This point is critical to becoming *Stress Teflon*; this is the fork in the stress road. You have to recognise when you are at the fork and engage your New Brain to take the high road. The high road is rational and thoughtful and finds solutions. The stress high road ensures that the situation is looked at objectively and your two brains remain integrated.

The low road is where the Old Brain is fired up and the New Brain reacts to the symptoms. 'I feel nervous. My heart's pounding.

Oh no, this must be bad.' This type of reaction is the New Brain being lazy. It also then feeds more stress into the Old Brain and amplifies its reactions. This is the stress feedback loop and it is part of the reason 18 per cent of the population suffers with anxiety or, worse still, panic attacks.[3]

This is not all bad; you just need to catch yourself heading down the low road and engage your New Brain to help solve the problem and not add fuel to the fire. Think of this as your '*Stress Teflon* off-ramp'—your way to avoid the feedback loop and find your

---

3   Stats from the Anxiety and Depression Association of America (ADAA).

way to a place where rational thinking helps solve your problems rather than amplifying them.

FORK IN THE STRESS ROAD

The psychiatrist and author Daniel Siegel outlines in his book *Mindsight* the hand model of the brain. I have adapted it a little bit to show you a really simple way to look at how our brains function.

In the following picture, or use your own hands, the left hand is the Old Brain and the right hand sits on the top and is the New Brain.

I want you to do an exercise for me. Make a fist with the left hand and put the right hand on top. A New-Brain-generated stress is like your right hand pushing down. Do that now and feel the tension in your chest and shoulders. This is what happens down the bad fork in the stress road. The New Brain creates tension, uses lots energy, and gets you nowhere.

Long-term anxiety is toxic stress and needs to be kept in check. The New Brain needs to take control, stop the feedback loop, and assess the situation from a rational and logical point of view. Unchecked anxiety causes health problems, unhappiness, and misery. These can be prevented by fully engaging the New Brain to put the issue into perspective.

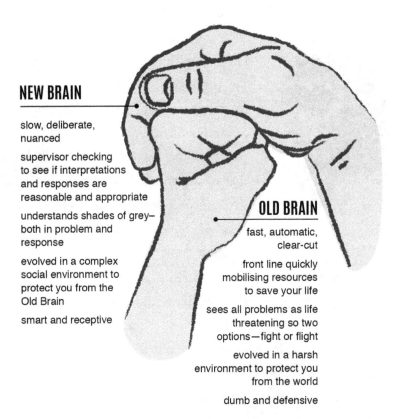

NEW BRAIN

slow, deliberate, nuanced

supervisor checking to see if interpretations and responses are reasonable and appropriate

understands shades of grey—both in problem and response

evolved in a complex social environment to protect you from the Old Brain

smart and receptive

OLD BRAIN

fast, automatic, clear-cut

front line quickly mobilising resources to save your life

sees all problems as life threatening so two options—fight or flight

evolved in a harsh environment to protect you from the world

dumb and defensive

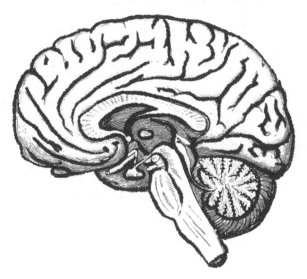

Make your brain model with your hands again. This time, gently pull upwards with your right hand. The tension in your chest disappears. *By using your New Brain to find solutions rather than creating the problems,* you decrease unwanted stress, put things in perspective, and go down the good fork in the stress road all the way to attaining *eudemonia* and becoming *Stress Teflon.*

How do we do this? We all know that telling yourself to calm down doesn't work. *Telling someone in an emotional state to calm down has the same effect as trying to baptise a cat.*

It never ends well. The Old Brain is in full-on reactive mode, amplified by a misdirected New Brain, and neither are going to simply calm down because you say so. If the New Brain is going to change its mind, it needs good reasons to do so, and the way to do that is to divert it from thinking about how you feel to thinking about the *actual situation.* You need to consciously assess the stressor.

First, a few slow deep breaths are always a great way to engage the *fight-or-flight* response's other half: the relaxation response. You can't take long, slow, deep breaths if you're being chased by a tiger. Deep breathing will take the edge off and allow you to move your thoughts from how you feel to what's really going on and assessing the situation, not the reaction.

Next, ask questions. Remember the Old Brain has no language. By asking questions, you have to engage your New Brain. Ask yourself, 'What am I thinking, why am I thinking it, and is it helping?' Answering these three simple questions truthfully will give you perspective, as these questions engage your supervising New Brain and can solve any problem rationally.

In really emotional situations, if these three questions don't do the trick and get the New Brain logical, you need a backup plan.

We know the Old Brain doesn't have a capacity for language. So it definitely can't do math. To get the New Brain on board, ask yourself—on a scale of one to ten, where one is a minor irritation and ten is completely horrible—how bad is the current situation? Be really honest. Think about other really bad things. Think about other not-so-bad things. Think about how things you've stressed about before have turned out. Think about how likely each of your imagined outcomes really is. Think about how bad this thing will really be in a month, three months, a year. Come up with a number and then think about it again. Is this really a reasonable number? If you are above an eight, and no one is dying, you aren't assessing very well.

Now, rate your response to the following questions, on a scale of one to ten: How bad do you feel? How much mental energy are you allocating to this situation? Is your response right now affecting your sleep, relationships, enjoyment, and health? Are your situation numbers and reaction numbers the same? Now just quietly think about those numbers for a bit, repeat as necessary, and calm the hell down.

Now, one-to-ten ratings might sound trivial or flippant, but the process does a number of things. Firstly, it distracts your New Brain from focusing on how you feel right now thereby breaking, at least temporarily, that feedback loop driving the *fight-or-flight* response. Secondly, it diverts the New Brain to assess the actual situation rather than your internal feelings, as it should have done in the first place. Most importantly, it gives your New Brain a reason that it came up with itself for turning the Old Brain down: 'I'm not just telling myself to calm down. I've assessed the situation and rationally determined that it's a three whilst my response is clearly a seven. Not only that, now that I think about it, I can deal with this.' Your New Brain needs reasons to do things. Sometimes it will accept bad reasons over good ones, but it hates doing things simply because you said so.

– CHAPTER 4 –
MIND AWARENESS

'The mind is its own place, and in itself can make heaven of hell, a hell of heaven.'

—John Milton, *Paradise Lost*

Buddha once was asked what he'd gained from meditation. His response might surprise you. He said, 'Nothing! However, let me tell you what I lost: anger, anxiety, depression, insecurity, fear of old age, and death.'

Science has shown the benefits of meditation and Buddha is right. It does all those things. The problem is, most of us are terrible at meditation. In the modern world of constant information overload and multitasking, being able to clear and reset the brain is a really valuable skill.

I have tried to meditate and clear the mind completely. I've even bought relaxation CDs that play sounds like dolphins farting or 'waterfall mist.' These either make me remember TV episodes of *Flipper* from the '70s or make me want to pee. I never manage to get meditation right. If I try to (*cue slow calming voice*) imagine a tranquil lake, before I know it, there are people surfing, bikini-clad women on the beach, and a long par five with a golf green on the lake's edge. I'm no good at meditation.

After reading Daniel Seigel's book *Mindsight*, I sort of adapted a different way of looking at meditation that gets rid of the you're-not-doing-it-right part. It's kind of like mindfulness, but I can't bring myself to use the word 'mindfulness'—too many images of soap-dodging hippies polluting my ears with dodgy renditions of 'Kumbuya.' For the purposes of this book and in the interests of becoming *Stress Teflon*, we are going to stay hippy-free and call it *mind awareness*.

Every morning when I wake up, I have five to ten minutes of mind awareness. You don't have to do anything special. Just lie however you are comfortable and breathe in through your nose and out through your mouth—nice and deep. As we said in chapter 2, deep breathing relaxes the Old Brain and allows your mind to go wherever it pleases. Don't restrain your thoughts. Just be aware of them. Don't judge them or find solutions to problems. Let them come to you freely, and when they do, reflect on them one by one by simply acknowledging them. It's just that easy. Try it. For the next two weeks, spend the first five minutes, after you wake up, breathing deeply through your nose, getting any tension out of the system, and allowing your thoughts to come in. Don't consciously judge them, because, remember, your Old Brain will judge things. Resist that urge, turn off the Old Brain, and just let the thoughts come through. Let them wander in one way and play around as long as they want, and then see what else comes into your brain. By spending five minutes doing that every morning, you will get stronger at identifying your thoughts. You'll also get better at understanding why you're having those thoughts and whether they're helping.

This process helps you identify your dominant thoughts and put them in perspective rather than letting them ruminate in your subconscious and rent a room in your head for free. We're hardwired, after all, to keep ruminating until we work out the problem.

Mind awareness is about understanding what you are thinking. It's only after you understand what you are thinking that you can begin to look at why you are thinking it and if it's helping. We're talking about how the brain *thinks* and how we perceive our reality as a result. As I touched on in the last chapter, the Old Brain can bully a weak and underused New Brain. The New Brain is the supervisor; it has to make sure that the Old Brain is kept in check. By simply stopping to take stock of the situation, mind awareness allows the New Brain to look at things rationally and then search for solutions.

When people get in a rut, they can grow more accepting of the Old Brain dictating what happens. They are being reactive. This can lead to helplessness, apathy, and depression. The correct type of stress can reverse this. Starting a new project, switching jobs, or learning a new skill can be stressful, but these actions get you out of your comfort zone and take you down the good fork in the stress road. In the words of the philosopher Taylor Swift: 'Shake it off!' If you don't like how things are going, do something. As the old line goes, if you always do what you've always done, you'll always get what you've always got. You need stress to get yourself out of a rut.

REIN THE BRAIN: LINKING OLD AND NEW BRAINS TOGETHER

Once you have an emotional reaction, whether it's a panic attack, a heated argument, or a moment of intense grief, your Old Brain is going to take over until you do something that tells it not to. In the hand model, it's like taking the top hand off and letting the Old Brain have free rein. That's not a bad thing if the situation warrants it, like the Tasmanian snake situation. In a matter of life and death, lightning-fast action is required and this is exactly when you want your Old Brain steering the ship.

What happens if your Old Brain steers the ship for too long? If the Old Brain dominates, the New Brain will eventually come back online, and rather than providing the practical wisdom needed for *eudemonia*, the New Brain simply finds a way to explain the Old Brain's reactions.

In the Hawaiian road rage incident, my errant finger triggered a response in machete man's Old Brain that said he was under threat. The New Brain then rationalised the reaction, amplified the Old Brain reaction, and made it okay to reach for the machete and our island friend was stuck in a stress feedback loop. Killing tourists isn't something that would align with his inner values, so somehow his New Brain needed to regain control. Fortunately his New Brain kicked in when he saw me as a husband and father, and he found a way to exit the loop before blood (mine) was shed.

To put it another way, let's say you're having an argument in which you decided to say something that was unkind and hurtful. Being mean and hurtful is not something that you would deliberately do. The reason you do something that's not in line with your inner values is because your New Brain has been bullied by the Old Brain into believing it's under siege. Suddenly, irrational thoughts and justifications spring into your mind, like 'Well, they did it to me, so I'm going to do this to them.'

Doing something you know is wrong and out of character is stressful and your brain will need to find a way to justify this. My mum used to say, 'Two wrongs don't make a right!' And she was right. Doing something you know you shouldn't is an example of cognitive dissonance. That regret-laced time bomb has a lot to do with a lack of mind awareness. We will have a larger look at cognitive dissonance and self-deception in chapter 9.

When your Old Brain has taken over during a false alarm, it has dumped loads of stress hormones into your system to engage the *fight-or-flight* response and regret is usually not far behind it. Your rational New Brain simply can't think clearly while you're in the middle of a stress response, so your Old Brain is called into action as the default. As we've said, the Old Brain focuses on the negative and is defensive and dumb. When this happens, you have to regain control of yourself, or else you could wake from your blind rage in hospital, in jail, unemployed, or divorced.

The biggest tool to help you rein in your Old Brain is breathing and mind awareness. As soon as you inhale and take nice, big, calm breaths, your body is telling your brain to relax: 'No, we've got this. Everything is under control. We're not getting chased by anything nasty. Life's not under threat.' You *can't* take big, deep breaths if you are being chased by a tiger and your life is under threat. It's not going to happen. If those tigers are imagined, you *can* take a few deep breaths, and those deep breaths are often all you need to get your head straight. So just by pausing for a second and breathing in deeply, the Old Brain dials down the emotions a little bit and gives your New Brain the freedom and clarity it needs to sort out the situation, using more complex thoughts. Remember the three questions: What am I thinking? Why am I thinking it? Is it helping? Only the New Brain can answer complex questions. Asking questions and answering them honestly is a great way to get the New Brain reattached and steering the ship.

Charlie Teo is an internationally renowned neurosurgeon who pioneered the use of keyhole brain surgery and minimally invasive neurosurgery. In an interview, he told the story of a particularly stressful operation.[4]

His patient was an internationally acclaimed pianist who happened to have a malignant brain tumour in the part of the brain that controls motor function—not ideal. Lots of neurosurgeons were saying the operation couldn't be done. Charlie was also being interviewed by a national television network, and there were cameras in the operating theatre. It was pretty stressful. During the procedure, Charlie found himself in a predicament and was losing control of the operation. Being a smart guy, he knew he had to stop and reassess the situation. So, in an attempt to find the best solution, he asked himself '*What John Wayne would do?*' I don't like the idea of a neurosurgeon taking advice from a cowboy, but I do love the way Dr Teo was self-aware enough to know he was in trouble. By asking himself a question, he managed to re-engage his New Brain and find a pathway out of a life-threatening situation.

You don't have to be a brain surgeon to know how to keep your two brains connected. I once witnessed a great example of the New Brain and Old Brain becoming disconnected, and I asked my fourteen-year-old daughter, Chloe, to write the story.

CHLOE'S ASSIGNMENT STORY

It was in the middle of the week and I had an English assignment due that morning. I admit it wasn't a great idea to print it out in the morning, but that's what I did. When I looked at the printout, it had cut out about five words from each line of writing. The computer

---

4 ABC Iview, 'Anh's brush with fame,' video, http://iview.abc.net.au/programs/anhs-brush-with-fame/DO1523H003S00.

wouldn't let me edit it and I had ten minutes before my 7:15 a.m. bus left. My teacher, Mr Perry (Mad Dog Perry, as we call him), was going to yell at me. This was not good. I was panicking. I couldn't breathe and I now had five minutes before the bus left.

I yelled out for Dad to help me, and he stated the obvious: that it was a stupid idea to leave it to the last minute. He started to give me a lecture about how you should always do it the night before. This definitely didn't help and Dad realised it. He told me not to worry about the bus; he would drive me to school.

That was one worry sorted. Dad held my hand and quietly told me to breathe. I didn't listen to him and continued to panic. All I could think of was how mad Mr Perry would be.

In the car on the way to school, we did some breathing exercises and I could feel my whole body relax and start to calm down. When I was calm, Dad and I talked about how I structured the assignment and we worked out the problem together. We managed to put my assignment on a new document in the right format and turn it in online. I had heaps of time to print a hard copy for my teacher and handed everything in ten minutes before class started.

That night Dad told me what was happening in my head and he taught me some breathing exercises to locate which parts of the brain I essentially need to handle situations like this.

When Chloe was in panic mode about the bus and Mr Perry's impending rant, her Old Brain was in charge. By breathing and consciously relaxing, she allowed the New Brain to come back online and sort out her computer issues. In panic mode, she was 'defensive and dumb.' She couldn't solve the problem and was only finding excuses. By taking the *Stress Teflon* off-ramp, the New Brain was back online, she was smart again, and she solved the problem.

We now know that Old Brain has no language. By asking questions you have to engage your New Brain. By answering the questions honestly, without rationalisations, your New Brain will once again take the reins and become a better supervisor. If you were to ask a well-trained New Brain, 'Why am I thinking this?', it would hopefully identify its own rationalisations and make better choices.

Both Chloe and Charlie had taken a fork in the stress road that was taking them to somewhere they didn't want to go. Fortunately, through mind awareness and integrating their two brains, they both managed to find a *Stress Teflon* off-ramp and used their New Brain to find solutions.

Catching yourself near the fork in the stress road is the key to avoiding bad stress. Mind awareness and understanding why you are thinking a certain way is the key to finding the off-ramp and integrating your two brains.

On the rare occasion I have been unhappy in my marriage, it has usually been a result of *me* being selfish and justifying my poor choices by blaming my wife. It is a lot easier for us to blame others than it is to accept our own wrongdoing. Mind awareness will help clarify this and decrease a lot of internal conflict by increasing self-awareness and accountability.

When you are faced with any situation, good or bad, your brain releases chemicals into specific synapses—those tiny gaps between nerve cells in the brain—to spur you into action. And when you know more about what's happening to your brain in moments of pleasure, pain, love, pride, or fear, the calmer you'll be when it happens and the better off you'll be because of it.

FORK IN THE STRESS ROAD

New Brain Stressors:
"What if..."

W hat
A m
I
T hinking?

OLD BRAIN
Fires up.

W. A. I. T.

LIFE

Pulse quickens, heart rate increases, palms sweaty, knot in the stomach

Old Brain Stressors:
Danger

NEW BRAIN Engaged. Gets shit done.
Rational, controlled, confident, excited.

Challenge Response

STRESS TEFLON

Stresses are dealt with quickly.
Stress response stops.

STRESS TEFLON OFF RAMP
Catch your stress response here.

Threat Response

STRESS FEEDBACK LOOP

NEW BRAIN
Registers the stress response. "This must be bad!"

NEW BRAIN
Amplifies the response from the Old Brain, and sends it back to the old brain which increases its stress response.

– CHAPTER 5 –

CARROTS AND STICKS: THE CHEMISTRY OF BEHAVIOUR

'Happiness is when what you think, what you say, and what you do are in harmony.'

—Mahatma Ghandi

The human body is run by a system of *carrots* and *sticks*. Think of a Mexican farmer and his stubborn donkey. Our clever hombre gets the mule moving by using a stick to dangle a carrot in front of its face. The carrot is there to entice us to do something that is beneficial and the stick is there to remind us when we don't. Stress is the stick!

The stick has two methods for motivating us: one is to hold the carrot out in front to move the donkey (yes, you are the donkey) in the desired direction; the other is to hit the donkey (i.e. you) to get it moving.

Stress can give us direction, and it certainly gets us moving. Just think, though, what would happen to the donkey if our stick-wielding friend continued to hit it constantly? It would run aimlessly, without direction, and probably buck the sadistic hombre off. This is how Western society is using stress: like a stick to beat us toward a destination. And that's why stress is getting such a bad rap. We need to use stress to give us direction, to send us to places that are beneficial and away from those that aren't.

For Cronk, stress was short term, a quick tap on the arse to get him moving and *then* help with direction.

Have a look at the graph below.

STRESS CURVE

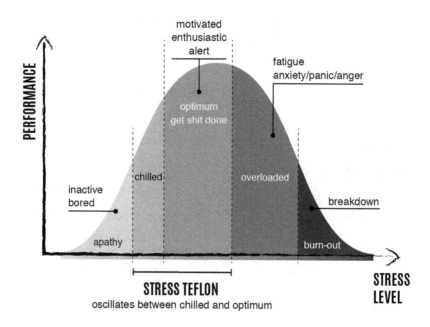

The far left of this curve is boredom and inactivity. Not much gets done, there are no challenges, and it's like week five on your quiet island holiday. You are bored shitless. The far right of the curve is where toxic stress takes over. The donkey is battered and bloodied and lying on the ground, unable to go anywhere (sorry about the imagery there).

The centre of the curve (chilled and optimum) is where the magic lies. This is where you get the best performance and you still have the ability to do more and get better. Most busy people are in this zone. They have the right type and amount of stress and they get shit done, as implied by the expression 'Give a busy person a job.'

Where are you on this curve? Are you too far left? You need to fire up. You may be in a rut and need some challenges. Find some positive stress, learn a new skill, change jobs, or set yourself a challenge.

A lot of people will say, 'I'm in the right side on this curve.' Are you really, and if so, where is that stress generated? Is it an overload of work challenges and things that need doing, or is it New-Brain-generated what-ifs? This is the key to becoming *Stress Teflon*: understanding where your stress comes from and working out ways to ensure stress is short-term and productive.

STICKS

What actually happens inside our bodies when we have a stress response? The star of the stress response is a chemical called cortisol.

Cortisol is responsible for a number of brain activities, but its relationship with epinephrine (or adrenaline) is what produces our *freeze-fight-or-flight* response. When Cronk faced off with a tiger, you can bet that heaps of cortisol was pouring into his reactive Old Brain telling him to react and act quickly.

Cortisol is what sets our priorities. When you have a *fight-or-flight* response to something, cortisol ensures you give that something your complete attention. With a tiger coming at him, Cronk was running totally on his Old Brain, and its super-fast reactions and increased strength (due to cortisol and adrenaline) saved the day. This is stress working at its beautiful, life-changing best.

You need a lot of energy to fight tigers, so, in a stroke of evolutionary genius, cortisol increases your heart rate. You breathe harder, which mobilises energy and oxygen and gets them to your muscles. All of these things are beneficial when fighting off tigers.

The other part of *fight or flight* is that cortisol turns off the systems in the body that aren't needed for fighting tigers. You don't need your hair to grow when you're fighting a tiger. You don't need your digestive and immune systems to work. Your lunch is irrelevant when you are about to become someone else's lunch. The New Brain goes offline and hands the reins to the faster reactions of the Old Brain. Mathematics and logical thinking aren't needed right now. Your body's repair and maintenance system takes a break. Basically, everything shuts down except the things needed to either fight or run.

Fight or flight is evolutionary genius in an environment where other beings want to kill us.

Today things are different. The tigers are in boardrooms and wear suits. The tigers are schoolyard bullies. The tigers are the threat of being homeless if you don't pay the rent. The tigers are modern fears, and most of them are generated in your New Brain: What if I lose my job? What if I fail my exams? What if my new business venture fails?

Cronk lived in the present. His tigers were very occasional. He dealt with them or he became lunch and didn't play any further part in the evolutionary process. Modern tigers are a different story. If your boss ignites a huge stress response, then he is your tiger. The modern tigers are in next office and will be a constant source of cortisol. Because most of our modern tigers are generated in our own heads, they can be constant or pop up whenever the New Brain fires up the Old Brain's stress response. Cortisol is a chemical. It doesn't care how it got there. It has a job to do. Shut down unnecessary systems and fire up the things we need to escape or fight.

So what happens if we have increased cortisol levels in the system for too long? Things shut down! Your immune system goes offline and you get sick. Not only do you get more colds and flus, but you open yourself up to an increased risk of things like cancer.

There is a school of thought that cancer is a failure of the immune system to deal with the offending cancerous cells. In situations of chronic stress, your immune system goes offline and it makes sense that these cancers are not dealt with very well. It's still early days, but there is a lot of research going into immunotherapy as a cancer treatment.[5]

Your digestive system fails to work and you get things like irritable bowel syndrome.

Your libido decreases. You are not going to get horny running away from tigers. If you feel you aren't getting enough love from your partner, perhaps you need to eliminate the things you do that add to your partner's stress levels. What are *you* doing that grinds your partner's gears and stresses her out? Stop doing it and be a bit more considerate and your partner will be more likely to get amorous. Apparently, nothing is sexier to a woman than a bloke vacuuming the house.

Now, I don't want to start worrying: 'OMG, I'm going to get cancer and IBS and never get laid again.' Stressing about stressing rarely helps. 'Worry, but know that worrying is about as effective

---

5   Cancer Research, UK, 'The immune system and cancer,' web page, http://www.cancerresearchuk.org/about-cancer/what-is-cancer/body-systems-and-cancer/the-immune-system-and-cancer.

as trying to solve an algebra equation by chewing bubble gum.'[6] Remember that it's only long-term chronic stress that is harmful to your health.[7] Short-term, power-boosting stress is actually beneficial. If you perceive stress as a positive thing that gets shit done, there are few negative health implications from it.

As Stanford scientist Kelly McGonigal says it's not the stress that kills you; it's your *perception* of stress that kills you. She cites a study that tracked thirty thousand people for eight years and found that 'people who experienced a lot of stress in the previous year had a 43 per cent increased risk of dying. But that was only true for the people who also believed that stress is harmful for your health. People who experienced a lot of stress but did not view stress as harmful were no more likely to die. In fact, they had the lowest risk of dying of anyone in the study, including people who had relatively little stress.'

It goes back to what she said earlier: chasing meaning is more beneficial than avoiding stress. Embrace the good stress and engage your New Brain to rationally put the bad stress into perspective. Remember that stress as a stick also gives us direction. It moves the carrot in the direction you want to go and away from places that will make us unsafe.

Pain is the other type of stick that our body uses. If something hurts, you stop doing it. This makes sense for harmful actions like sticking your hand in a fire and walking on broken glass, but what about pain's role in our relationships with other people? Like Cronk, humans are safer, happier, and more content when in a tribe. You are more likely to obtain the objective flourishing of *eudemonia* when you are in your tribe. We'll look closely at tribes in chapter 7.

---

6   Quindon Tarver, 'Everybody's Free to Wear Sunscreen,' song, 1997.

7   Kelly McGonigal, 'How to make stress your friend', TED, https://www.ted.com/talks/kelly_mcgonigal_how_to_make_stress_your_friend/transcript?language=en.

When you are excluded from your tribe, your brain literally feels pain. It's not just your figurative heart that hurts after a breakup or job termination. Turns out, your brain feels it in a very real way.[8] To test the theory, researchers met with subjects who had just split up in a relationship, probably our most intimate sort of tribe. Not surprisingly, they found them to be quite stressed and really miserable. Turns out the '60s pop song was right: breaking up really is hard to do; it hurts. The researchers gave half their broken-hearted subjects Tylenol and a placebo to the other half. Within a few days, the people who had received Tylenol were a lot happier than the people who hadn't received the pain reliever. Why? Because Tylenol, or paracetamol, works both at the site of the pain and in the brain. By giving the subjects Tylenol, researchers were dulling the natural pain of being separated from your tribe and actually made people feel better.

From this, it would appear that we have evolved to do things that will keep us in the tribe. What sort of things might get us kicked out of our tribe? Usually it's being selfish and putting ourselves before the tribe. Being an arsehole is stressful. It hurts and may get us kicked out of the tribe. Our biology tells us not to be like that.

CARROTS

Many different chemicals are released in our bodies. These are the carrots that feel good and make us repeat desirable behaviour. If you want a pigeon to walk in circles, you give it some seed every time it turns right. Pretty soon, the bird will turn right and dance in circles. The carrots in our biology are the same. Something feels good and

---

8   Kirsten Weir, 'The pain of social rejection', *Monitor on Psychology* 43, no. 4 (April 2012), http://www.apa.org/monitor/2012/04/rejection.aspx.

we'll do it again. Stress dangles the carrots out in front of us and takes us to the place where things feel good.

Carrot 1: Dopamine–Your Drive to Thrive

The first of our feel-good chemicals is dopamine, our drive-to-thrive hormone.

You probably won't hear about any brain chemical more than dopamine. It's the rock star of our brain because it's basically involved in all things sex, drugs, and rock 'n' roll. What I mean is dopamine reacts in our brain during sexual arousal, drug usage (particularly cocaine), and the pleasure we derive from getting something we want. Dopamine is a cue chemical, meaning it can tip us off that pleasure is coming our way. When Cronk hunted, as soon as he found his prey's trail, he got a hit of dopamine. As he got close and saw the animal, he got another hit. We get a hit of dopamine because our brain is predicting that a reward is coming. When Cronk threw his spear and killed the animal, he knew he had that night's dinner and he got a massive hit of dopamine. It felt great! Lets do it again tomorrow.

Being our drive-to-thrive hormone, dopamine is responsible for making us get better at things. It keeps us focused on the prize and the promise of a dopamine hit makes us more tenacious about getting what we want. For that reason, dopamine is often associated with addiction. Alcohol, gambling, work, mobile phones, sex, food, cocaine, *Game of Thrones*, coffee, smoking, chocolate, video games—the list is endless—are all things we can get addicted to and all of them recruit dopamine. Something felt good last time. I want it again.

Part of our stress response is adrenaline. We have all heard of adrenaline junkies, people who love extreme sports, jump out of perfectly good planes, or surf massive waves. They all have a love of adrenaline and the cue chemical dopamine is the one that tells them that it's on the way. It's addictive.

Do you love it when deadlines are approaching and you get fired up to get shit done? Is the New-Brain-generated drama in your life something you are actually addicted to? Is the combination of adrenaline and dopamine making you move from one drama to the next? By understanding dopamine addiction, integrating the two brains and practicing mind awareness, we can use the drive-to-thrive hormone for good rather than becoming a slave to it.

Scientists at Cambridge University and the University of Nottingham looked at the problem of gambling. What they discovered was that a near miss (four out of five on a slot machine) produced more dopamine than actually winning money.[9] Game designers understand this and deliberately put in more near misses to give people the cue chemical dopamine and keep them feeling good and on the game longer.

When it comes to gambling, dopamine can be a problem. For Cronk, the drive-to-thrive hormone was what kept him practicing his hunting skills as a young man. Every time he *nearly* got the bird, he got a feel-good hit of dopamine to make him keep practicing. Without dopamine, he would never have become the great hunter he was and humans would not have thrived.

Dopamine is great. But it's addictive and it needs to be kept in check. It's a short-term, feel-good hit that needs to get another one straight after. Hit your sales target, you get a bigger sales target.

---

9   Henry W. Chase and Luke Clark, 'Gambling severity predicts midbrain response to near-miss outcomes', *Journal of Neuroscience* 30, no. 20 (May 2010).

Got a good job, want a better job. Got good grades, want to get better grades. Dopamine is productive and essential but it never *fully* satisfies. It's a bit like Chinese food: an hour after the meal and you are hungry again.

Dopamine feels good and makes us happy in the short term. The problem is if you attach happiness to results, you will never truly get there. As the Harvard positive psychologist Shawn Achor says, 'If happiness is on the opposite side of success, your brain never gets there. We've pushed happiness over the cognitive horizon, as a society. And that's because we think we have to be successful, then we'll be happier.'[10] To achieve *eudemonia*, you have to choose to be happy first, and success will follow. Don't let happiness be something that relies on ticking all your dopamine boxes. There will always be more boxes and happiness will forever stay just over the horizon.

Carrot 2: Serotonin–Pride from the Inside

 Serotonin is your pride-from-inside hormone. There are few things better than taking a shot of serotonin to the brain. This is the chemical you get any time you do something well. It's the feeling of pride. It makes you feel good about yourself and makes you feel like a valued member of the tribe. Scoring the winning goal, nailing the presentation at work, making a group of friends laugh—anything that gives us a warm fuzzy feeling inside is usually being influenced by serotonin. It feels like weeing in a wetsuit. Every surfer knows the winter joy of peeing in a wetsuit. It feels great.

---

10   Shawn Achor, 'The happy secret to better work', TED, https://www.ted.com/talks/shawn_achor_the_happy_secret_to_better_work/transcript?language=en.

Standing on the top step at an Olympic medal ceremony or getting a Nobel Prize would be a source of great pride and at these times the winners are euphoric and so proud of themselves. Have you ever noticed their speeches are always about who got them there? 'I couldn't have done it without my coach (husband/mum/team)', they say. The camera moves over to the coach, head tilted to the side, big smile, nodding, and looking proud as punch. That's serotonin. It feels great and all it requires is that you do something you are proud of. You can't achieve *eudemonia* without serotonin. To objectively flourish, you have to feel proud of yourself and *like being you*. Pride from inside is the key to *eudemonia* and it's an essential piece of the *Stress Teflon* puzzle.

When I wanted to have a closer look at serotonin, I thought I'd talk to someone who was intimate with serotonin and the *pride from inside* that comes from achieving great things. I had a chat with Robbie McEwan.

Robbie is one of Australia's best-known cyclists and has travelled the world winning three Tour de France green jerseys and loads of other major races. If anyone could give me an insight into getting to the top of the tree and being proud of that achievement, it should be Robbie.

When I asked Robbie which wins in his cycling career he was most proud of, he thought for a while and told me two stories.

In the 2005 Tour de France, at stage thirteen, Robbie found himself in the peloton, nine minutes behind a breakaway of five strong riders, as they came out of the mountains. He'd already won a couple of stages in the tour, so when he and his teammates realised the breakaway was a long way ahead, Robbie said to them, 'I feel good, but it's up to you. We don't have to catch them if you don't want to.'

Despite being tired, his Lotto teammates decided they wanted the win and they worked their collective butts off to get it. They dragged the entire peloton, including Robbie, who rode tucked safely behind them, and caught the last two riders of the breakaway with two hundred metres to go. Showing his usual cunning and freakish acceleration, Robbie's last remaining teammate, Fred Rodriguez, took the last left-hander nice and wide and gave Robbie a clear view of the finish line. If he were good enough, he would win the sprint. He was.

'I was a few metres out from the line and I wanted to see if anybody was on my wheel, because I was actually going to let Freddy cross the line first', Robbie said. Freddy was spent and Robbie won the stage.

Usually, at the end of the stage, the rider leaves the finishing area to deal with the media and hydrate before going off to celebrate atop the podium. After finishing this race, though, Robbie stayed close to the finish line to welcome all of his teammates. There were hugs and maybe even a few tears. And although the record books show it was Robbie McEwan who won, he knows it was really his team.

His second most memorable win was in the 2007 Tour de France, in stage one. He crashed with twenty kilometres to go. His entire team waited for him as the peloton raced into the distance. Bruised, battered and bleeding, he got back on the bike and rejoined his waiting teammates. With Robbie safely behind them, the team pinned back their ears and started the difficult chase to catch the peloton.

They caught the peloton and Robbie hid in the pack until the last few hundred metres, where he once again sprinted to the front to claim the stage win.

What strikes me most after talking to Robbie is that both of his most memorable victories were not so much to do with him but with how good his team was. It shows us the power of being part of a group and how it is so much more important than individual accomplishments.

Talk about Robbie's passion: he still had shivers up his spine when recounting the Herculean work his teammates did. He loves talking about how several of his teammates had ten-year and fifteen-year careers and earned truckloads of money but were names not even diehard cyclists could readily recount. He was the star, but he attributes the biggest wins of his career to his teammates and the pride in his team. Serotonin needs other people and is the reason why team pride feels better than personal pride.

Fortunately, you don't have to win Olympic gold, Tour de France stages, or Nobel prizes to get serotonin. You just have to do something you are proud of.

One day, I was driving to the gym and was stopped at a set of traffic lights. An elderly gentleman with a walking stick and a bag of KFC was walking diagonally through the intersection. Lost and dis-orientated, he stopped in the middle of the lights and looked around, unsure which way to go. The lights were about to go green and I was very concerned that the old guy would get run over. My lane got a green light and I drove around him to block any cars coming the other way (when their lights turned).

When I enquired if he was okay, he looked at me with a tear in his eye and said, 'No, I'm a bit lost.'

'Jump in, mate', I said. 'I'll get you home.' With that, he got in the car and breathed a big sigh of relief. We got out of the intersection and found a safe place to park.

It turns out his name was Jack and he had gone out to get lunch for himself and his wife about four hours earlier. Coming out of KFC, he had turned right instead of left and had been walking all that time.

Fortunately, Jack knew his address. We drove the six kilometres back to his house and finally delivered lunch to his very hungry wife. Jack and I had a great chat in the car and I was really glad that I could help. This one little act of kindness felt great. I was flooded with serotonin's *pride from inside* and felt great because I'd helped someone.

Why don't we do these things more often? They feel fantastic. Hold the door open for someone, help a struggling mum get the pram in her car, or let people go in front of you in traffic. These things are all a source of serotonin. They make you happier about what sort of person you are. Pride from inside. We should all do more things like this.

Both serotonin and dopamine feel great. The big difference between them is that you *can't* get serotonin by yourself. To truly get *pride from inside*, you need other people. Robbie's greatest wins weren't about him. They were about the team. In fact, you don't even need to do anything. You can get serotonin from seeing other members of your tribe succeed. The joy you feel when your daughter gets her diploma—that's serotonin. Your son hits a home run—serotonin. A novice staff member uses her newfound knowledge to help a customer; you both get serotonin and it feels awesome.

Recently, I caught up with my friend Alan Hopkins (Hoppy). Within seconds, he was telling me about his eldest son, David, who had had played guitar and sung at his school concert the night before. Hoppy pulled out his phone and played me part of the performance. It sounded great, but what I loved was how excited and proud Hoppy was of his son. I got a little hit of serotonin too. Serotonin is contagious and you get it by doing things and being part of your tribe, just like Cronk.

Carrot 3: Oxytocin–Tend and Befriend

Some call it the love drug, while others (including me) refer to it as your tend-and-befriend hormone. Oxytocin is the carrot that feels good when we have physical contact with people we care about. Get a hug from your mum and you get oxytocin. Footballers hug after they score a goal—oxytocin (and serotonin). It's why we shake hands at the end of a deal negotiation: it creates bonds. Childbirth would be horrendously painful, but the massive hit of oxytocin a mother receives when she first holds her baby nullifies the pain when the new mum bonds with her child. You get a flood of oxytocin when you have an orgasm. Remember, evolution ensures the carrots make us repeat things that feel good. How often would you have sex (and reproduce) if an orgasm felt like slamming your genitals in a car door? The species would have been extinct years ago. Oxytocin helps us feel safe, reduces anxiety, and lets us know when we belong.

We look at oxytocin as a carrot that brings us together and creates bonds with the people we care about. But there are a couple of different sides to it. *Oxytocin is actually part of your stress response.* From an evolutionary point of view, in times of danger, it makes us want to be close to people we care about. Oxytocin creates bonds between people and generally makes us feel safe.

Men who have been to war together have a bond that lasts a lifetime. Thanks to your tend-and-befriend carrot, stress can bring people together.

A number of years ago, I went scuba diving. I had never been before, so I did the little one-day course in the pool and we went out to the Great Barrier Reef. There's beautiful coral everywhere. We were just ten or fifteen metres underwater, swimming along in a group of about five or six, when we looked up and saw a reef shark.

I knew what a reef shark was, and I know they don't typically attack people. But this shark was as big as me. It had big, sharp teeth and I'm pretty sure if it had wanted to attack me, I'd have been proper fucked. But I found myself just swimming over to the instructor and staying shoulder to shoulder with him. I was scared because I was in uncharted territory, with sharks no less, but as soon as I had the physical touch, even if it was through a wetsuit, I calmed down immediately. Oxytocin is part of the stress response and part of the stress relief.

I used to be of the opinion that people who blamed their fucked-up mental health on their parents or their childhood were full of shit and should just get over it. It was history. When I began looking at neural pathways, I realised just how wrong I was.

If, like me, you were bought up in a loving, caring environment, your tend-and-befriend hormones work as they were designed. They bring you closer to the people in your tribe to help deal with a stressful situation. If your memories aren't positive, oxytocin release can have a negative effect, making love, relationships, and bonding really difficult.

In the 1980s, just after the end of the Cold War, reporters discovered that orphanages in Romania had been run in such a way as to limit physical touch to the children there. Because they had been denied much love and affection, the majority of the orphans had never experienced the positive sensation that oxytocin causes. Their tiny body had produced oxytocin, but they didn't get the physical touch that made them feel safe. To them, oxytocin was *not* something that made them feel safe; it reminded them of being alone and vulnerable. So they actually had an adverse reaction to touch or any attempt to bond with them that caused an oxytocin release. When their neural pathways were being created, they may have reached out for love and caring but didn't get that loving attention.

If we cast our mind back to chapter 3 and think of our neural pathways as tracks in the sand dunes, the Romanian orphans had pathways and memories that equated oxytocin only with sadness. In this case, oxytocin, as part of the stress response, sent them completely the other way, pushing them away from people and from love to somewhere much darker. They had no association between the tend-and-befriend hormone and feeling safe.

Some confronted their discomfort through consistent and controlled exposure therapy, but the fact that they still struggled with a number of psychological deficiencies led researchers to understand more about the importance of brain chemicals like oxytocin in stimulating the brain and developing healthy, normal relationships.

Your tend-and-befriend hormone is a positive carrot that makes most people closer and the tribe better.

Carrot 4: GABA—Calm and Disarm

Then there's GABA (or gamma-aminobutyric acid, for the nerds) that strange-sounding goop that's actually an amino acid and is your calm-and-disarm carrot. GABA is a neurosuppressor, which means it's a natural calming agent, released in the central nervous system to suppress nerve transmissions and thereby reduce nervousness. You may see bottles of GABA for sale at your local health foods store, typically advertising it as some type of all-natural tranquilizer. Whereas adrenaline is your accelerator, GABA is your brakes. Exercises like tai chi, yoga, and meditation all have the effect of releasing GABA. I like to think of GABA as being like a fire extinguisher that can cover the brain with calm, cooling foam and put out any number of brain-generated spot fires. Breathing is the key to releasing it and you can do it consciously. In times of intense emotions, all it takes is a bit of vertical integration between your Old and New Brains and breathing deliberately. Your New Brain can generate fires or it can put them out. Your calm-and-disarm chemicals help put fires out.

Don't worry. I know that's a lot to remember, so I crafted a handy cheat sheet, rhymes and all, for you to help you retain all you need to know about brain chemicals:

- Cortisol/adrenaline: *freeze, fight, and flight*

- Dopamine: *drive to thrive*

- Serotonin: *pride from inside*

- Oxytocin: *tend and befriend*

- GABA: *calm and disarm*

– CHAPTER 6 –
STRESS INDUCERS

'If you knew you could handle anything that came your way, what would you possibly have to fear? The answer is: nothing!'

—**Susan Jeffers,** *Feel the Fear and Do It Anyway: Dynamic Techniques for Turning Fear, Indecision and Anger into Power, Action and Love*

Do you think Cronk would have had a fear of tigers?

Absolutely, they have massive teeth, big claws, and can run really fast. Cronk, like us, had small teeth, tiny nails, and soft skin and was nowhere near as fast. Cronk would have been shit-scared of tigers and so he should.

Let's think for a moment about how Cronk would have handled his fear when he had an encounter with a hungry tiger. Obviously, it was a really stressful moment, and it's likely that he would have had the same initial reaction any of us would have under the same circumstances. His heart would have been racing, his breathing would have quickened, and a sense of urgent panic would have spread throughout his body. He would have been scared, but he would have used only his Old Brain to react. Everything he did in that moment would have been instinctive—100 per cent Old Brain. He wouldn't have thought anything through. He would have done exactly what he had to do to kill the tiger and protect himself and his tribe.

But as soon as he had killed the tiger, the stress would have gone away. He would have breathed deeply and celebrated his victory with all of his tribe, embracing the people around him. He would have hugged his fellow hunters and said, 'Fuck me. We just got attacked by a tiger.' Embracing others and breathing deeply provides a trigger that tells your Old Brain to *calm and disarm*. It's a cue to stop producing adrenaline/cortisol and cease the *fight-or-flight* reaction. Surviving a really stressful situation gives us great pride and a massive hit from all our good carrot feelings. It's like the old saying that whatever doesn't kill you makes you stronger. Caveman stressors are obvious to see and have a beginning and end. Conquering your fears builds your pride in yourself and becomes the foundations of self-belief.

'You gain strength, courage, and confidence by every experience in which you really stop to look fear in the face. You are able to say to yourself, "I lived through this horror. I can take the next thing that comes along."'

—Eleanor Roosevelt

We have stress so that if we are attacked by a tiger, we react quickly to ensure our survival. Stress saved Cronk, and it saves us from so many things we face in our lives. But as we keep saying, stress is designed to be really short and intermittent.

Fear is our main stress inducer and almost all fears can come back to one general fear: *fear that we can't handle a particular situation.*

A feeling of being overwhelmed is a type of stress that sparks the fear that we can't handle a situation. Having lots of balls in the air can be overwhelming and make you feel you can't handle a situation. You can! You just need to stay rational, keep your two brains connected, and find creative ways to solve the problems. Being overwhelmed is your cue to ask for help. The stress response of oxytocin tells us to look for people to help. Listen to your own rewards system and ask people to help.

WHAT-IFFING AND RED SPLATS

A mate of mine is afraid of heights. 'I get nervous on thick-piled carpet', he told me. He's *really* afraid of heights. Somehow his fourteen-year-old son conned him into abseiling down a high-rise building in the centre of town. So there he is, on a ledge twenty stories up, and he's absolutely freaking out while his son is calm as a cucumber. My mate turns to his son and says, 'You're not even nervous. Why aren't you worried about this?', to which his son replied, 'Dad, come over here. Go on over to the edge of the building. Look down.'

My mate, still petrified, manages to step to the edge.

'People have been doing this all day', his son tells him. 'They've raised thousands of dollars. Fifty people have done this before us. Have a look down at the bottom. Do you see any red splats on the pavement?'

He looked over the railing and gazed at the site below for a moment. 'No, there are no red splats there.'

'These people know what they're doing. All we've got to do is climb down the rope and we're fine.'

Suddenly, it made him calm down and he was okay. He realized the tiger he had created in his head was actually only in his head. He knew they had safety procedures. He knew what to do. He just had to use his New Brain to *calm and disarm* his Old Brain. Then he'd be able to think rationally and function well. As soon as he thought rationally, he realized everything was safe and professional and they would be fine. Together, they abseiled down the face of the building to the ground, where they celebrated my mate's conquest of his greatest fear.

That story is an example of how we develop our own tigers. They are New-Brain-generated fears and all of them stem from the fear that we can't handle the situation. We almost always can.

How many red splat fears (fear that something bad might happen) do you have in your life? The psychiatrist Robert Leahy calls this type of thinking what-iffing. He cites a study in which scientists got subjects to list the things they were worried about and then looked the number of these imagined calamities that never eventuated. They came up with 85 per cent. This means that only about one in every seven of your red splats actually happens. Even more telling than that, the study also showed that for the 15 per cent of things that actually did happen to the participants, 79 per cent of them handled the situation better than they had expected and looked at the situation as a 'lesson worth learning.'[11] This means that only one in thirty-three of your worries are actually going to happen and affect your life in a negative way. With stats like that, how much of your what-iffing now seems pretty unproductive?

If you stop and engage your New Brain and ensure the vertical integration that we talked about in chapter 3, you really engage your brain's supervisor. It can release GABA, which will have a calming influence on the Old Brain.

---

11   Robert L. Leahy, *The Worry Cure*, New York: Potter/TenSpeed/Harmony, 2005.

THE WORRY PIE

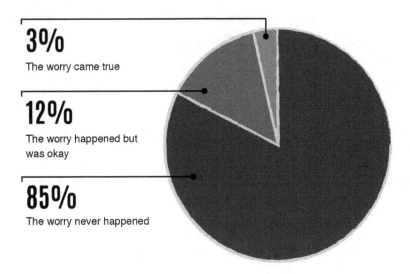

3%
The worry came true

12%
The worry happened but
was okay

85%
The worry never happened

Fear rears its ugly, stress-inducing head in so many ways. Fear of failure and fear of change are two particularly insidious stress inducers that stop people from achieving *eudemonia*. Both of these two fears are capable of turning talented, creative, and motivated people into apathetic sheep that never leave their comfort zone. Mind awareness is a great way to identify the fears you have that may be holding you back. If you are truly honest when you answer the question 'Why you are thinking…' in terms of fear, you will invariably get to the root of your fear.

DISAPPOINTMENT

*'If you align expectations with reality,
you will never be disappointed.'*

— Tyrell Owens, NFL champion

Disappointment is a major stress inducer in a number of ways. The most obvious one is when people let you down. It's not unrealistic to have expectations of people and when they fail to live up to them, it is stressful. You feel let down, unimportant, and unappreciated. How much of those negative emotions are the fault of *your* expectations and placing *your* priorities on someone else? Parents get stressed yelling at their children for many things, such as not cleaning their rooms. Whether they realise it or not, the source of that stress is often the parents' own expectations. They think their children should have more respect, look after their things, and keep their room tidy. It's a parent's job to teach kids good habits. If doing so causes fights, stress, and friction in the family, perhaps the parents need to find a different, more effective way to get their point across. By staying rational, you are a lot more likely to find a solution than with confrontation and yelling.

Road rage is a great example of disappointment causing stress and firing up the Old Brain and causing calm, rational people to lose their shit. We all know the road rules and have an expectation that everyone else will follow them. When the muppet in front of you is too busy texting on his phone to notice the traffic lights have gone green, you are well within your rights to yell abuse and let your Old Brain give him a spray. But does it really matter if that driver's inattention makes you two minutes late? Probably not. Put that stuff in perspective. It's not the end of the world.

Similarly, dangerous drivers really fire up the Old Brain. Cars can kill people and young kids weaving in and out of the traffic in hotted-up cars and with their hats on backwards cause an Old Brain reaction that is designed to keep us alive in the jungle. The New Brain coming in and throwing fuel on the fire probably doesn't help, but it's what happens to a lot of people. Use your New Brain for good and decrease the rage, not fuel it.

Not meeting your own expectations—letting yourself down—can be an even bigger stress inducer. I have a line I often use: *no one disappoints me like I disappoint myself.*

I say it as a joke, often after doing something stupid or when waking up after a big night. These disappointments are usually just funny or embarrassing and don't really cause too much stress. Any time I attempt a DIY project, these feelings will almost invariably pop up. When I do a good DIY job, it's like a blind squirrel finding an acorn and it feels great, but overall I full-heartedly admit that I'm crap at DIY. My wife calls me Bob the Breaker. It will take four holes to hang one picture and, even then, I can guarantee it won't be straight. But I don't let the things that I'm crap at define me. Thankfully, I am good at other things and my faulty DIY gene is one of those crap things about me I accepted years ago. The family still gets nervous when the tools come out, though.

Imagine a work situation in which one of your employees failed to do something he or she was responsible for and your company lost a big contract. You would be upset and disappointed. Your natural response would be to tear five shades of shit out of the staff member who fucked up. Yelling and screaming won't help much, but that's what a lot of bosses do. Losing your shit at staff members rarely helps. It creates a stressful environment, and we know that when stressed, people become defensive and dumb—hardly a good way to navigate a difficult situation. It's not effective.

Initially, losing your temper might feel good because you get the frustration out, but after the dust settles and you reflect on your actions, you always feel disappointed that you didn't handle the situation better. Flipping your lid, losing your shit, and separating your two brains is a great way to create stress from regret.

The problem is that disappointment and regret are useless, stressful emotions that don't achieve much. By integrating the Old and New Brains, you can prevent your mistakes and hopefully learn from them when they do occur. Learning from mistakes can decrease the stress hormones you are generating and can even create some *pride from inside* that will help you stop beating yourself up.

Karen, my wife, started smoking on a church retreat at the age of thirteen. Like all new teenage smokers, she coughed and spluttered her way through the first few ciggies. She persisted because the opportunity to feel grown up was worth the bad breath and threat of lung cancer. This was the '80s in Ireland and everyone smoked. People smoked in pubs and in their houses, and there were even smoking sections on planes. Twenty years later, times had changed. The health effects of smoking were now conclusive and it had become socially taboo to blow smoke near anyone. Fortunately, pregnancy and a new baby had kept her off the butts for over a year, but, somehow, she managed to get back on the cancer sticks, and before she knew it, she was a smoker again. She was massively disappointed in herself and, in spite of me busting her chops about it, she continued to smoke for a few more years.

The penny finally dropped, and she gave up the cancer sticks once and for all, largely because she was sick of disappointing herself and beating herself up for doing something she knew was unhealthy and setting a bad example for her daughter. As of now, she hasn't smoked in over four years and she ranks giving up smoking as one of the things she is proudest of.

POOR HEALTH

As we discussed in chapter 2, Ragsy's health scare induced a lot of stress for a lot of people. Remember stress is there to keep us alive. It directs us away from things that hurt and toward things that feel good. The hassle with modern life is that there are heaps of things that feel great but aren't so good for you. Chocolate, fast food, alcohol, and drugs all stimulate the production of dopamine and feel good *at the time*. As we've heard, these things can be quite addictive and are often the cause of many health problems. The recent epidemics of diabetes, obesity, and depression can, at least in part, be attributed to chronic bad stress.

We now know that cortisol shuts down unnecessary systems in the body, but the other part of the *fight-or-flight* response is what it does to sugar, insulin, and fat. When Cronk saw a tiger, his heart rate went up, his breathing quickened, and his liver put extra sugar into the bloodstream to give him the energy and strength he needed to fight or run. Sounds like a good system right? It worked for Cronk.

What about our modern, New-Brain-generated, chronic stress? It has the same chemical process going on. The only problem is we aren't running anywhere or fighting anyone so the sugar that was made available to run or fight doesn't get used. What happens to this extra energy in the blood stream? It gets stored as fat, usually near the liver, as abdominal fat.

BRAIN BOX

Stress, sugar, fat: the vicious circle

The stress hormone cortisol signals the liver to liberate its glucose (sugar) stores. To fight or flee, the body needs energy and cortisol gets our body ready for action. In the past, those sugars would have been used to run or fight. Today the stressors rarely require any physical movement and, eventually, the increased sugar in the system will signal the pancreas to make more insulin. The liver doesn't detect sugars, but it does react to insulin by removing the sugar from the blood stream, converting it to fat, and storing it nearby. This causes abdominal fat and it is the reason that a lot of people who suffer chronic stress are overweight and have higher incidence of diabetes.

Chronic stress makes most people crave bad food. No one has ever come home after a hard day at work and excitedly said, 'I really *need* some celery sticks and fat-free humus.' Stress makes you want fat, sugar, and junk food. You need energy to fight your stress tigers. The hassle with these foods is that they are going into a system that already has high sugar levels due to cortisol. High-calorie stress foods then fuel the stress-sugar-insulin-fat loop that is making a lot of modern Westerners overweight.

Graham Bendeich was an athlete, a coach, and a businessman. Somewhere in his midforties the businessman part of his life started to dominate his life. Fourteen-hour days, high-stakes deals, and long lunches saw his slight frame blow out to over a hundred kilograms (220 lb.). He was unfit. There was no time to exercise, and he was not feeling too good about himself. Business was thriving, but he didn't have *eudemonia*, he didn't have balance, and he wasn't happy. Around this time, he stopped and had a look at his life. 'What would I pay to be seventy-five kilograms again?' he asked. This one question got his New Brain thinking. He came up with a number: $1 million! He would pay a million dollars to weigh seventy-five kilograms again. That's how important it was to him. Graham decided to step away from the parts of his business that took up a lot of time and caused chronic stress. It cost him a lot of money, but it was worth it. Within six months, he was back down to his fighting weight and his life had balance again.

STRESS AND POSTURE

It may sound strange, but stress has some very close ties to our posture. There's actually a two-way link between your brain and your body, which researchers have begun to correlate with an increase in anxiety disorders in children.

Don't believe me? Let's say you were in the jungle and there were life-and-death threats all around you. You get small to hide and/or protect yourself. You pull your elbows in. You pull your knees up to your chest. You'd get somewhere safe and you'd hide, which is a natural response. It's what little kids will do if they get scared. If you watch little kids, they'll go in the corner and make themselves as small as they can when they're afraid or upset.

Dogs will do the same thing. If you come in with a big, powerful voice and you say to your dog, 'You just shat on the rug', the dog will go down and get small. The dog has no clue what 'shat on the rug' means. He just knows you are pissed and wants out of your way. It's a natural response. It's part of the freeze response. You get small.

Researchers are even discovering that because kids are spending so much time on their phone, their posture and their body language is actually telling them that they're under threat because they're posture is shrunken. Their body inadvertently takes a defensive position, which triggers an anxiety response in their brain. *Remember that we've got that two-way reaction between our body and brain.* That posture you adopt when you hunch over and bring your elbows in close and you look at your phone all the time is actually causing the Old Brain to feel vulnerable and nervous as if you were weak, powerless, and under threat.

What they're noticing, though, is if you can get kids, or anyone for that matter, to sit up straight, move away from their computers periodically, put their shoulders back, and open their bodies up, their brain doesn't produce those anxiety-based hormones and they feel much more at ease throughout the day.

I recently met someone who is an expert in this area. Dr Arne Rubinstein has dedicated his life to studying adolescent development. He's a part-time ER doctor and a full-time advocate for children. He serves as the founder and CEO of the Making of Men organization. He is a counsellor and the author of the popular book *The Making of Men: Raising Boys to be Happy, Healthy, and Successful.* He has a real concern that kids are being prescribed antidepressants at around the age of nine or ten. This is horrific. Arne suggests a common-sense approach to combatting the use of drugs on children: take their devices away from them and make them go outside and play. Doing so makes them use their muscles, burn up nervous energy, and stimulates their mind in a more balanced way than does sitting in front of an artificial stimulant like a TV or a computer. Just by being physically active, children are getting their body to say, 'No. I'm bigger. I'm stronger. I'm not under threat.' And that simple sense of control and safety helps them think more clearly and develop psychologically and physically in a more balanced way.

In times of stress, I love the idea that posture can actually influence the brain's reactions. I do a thing I call being big and breathe: I sit up tall, shoulders back, arms out, and have a few really big, deep breaths. By being big and breathing, your body is telling your brain that it's not under threat, the stress isn't going to harm you or kill you, and you're okay. That turns off your cortisol response, your HPA axis, and allows your New Brain to calm your Old Brain and *calm and disarm* your stress response. It turns off all of that stress response because you can't stand in front of a tiger, put your arms out wide, and be big and brave. It's just not going to happen.

If you're creating your own tigers in your head, the way to deal with them is by stretching out. That's why things like yoga are so good. In yoga you spend a lot of time stretching and making yourself longer. Tai chi also involves a lot of these stretches. You're breathing in really deeply. What that tells your brain is that you're not under any threat. You couldn't stand out in the jungle with lions all around and do tai chi. It's not going to happen. But in our modern world it's using that two-way connection between mind and body to tell your brain you're big, strong, and okay. Kids hunkering over an iPad are indirectly telling themselves that they're small, vulnerable, and under threat.

Simply put, what you do with your posture actually tells your brain how it should react. That's why practices such as mind awareness exercises that focus on stopping, breathing deeply, stretching, and telling your brain that you're okay are so helpful in turning off your stress responses. If you're playing a violent or scary video game, for instance, you are triggering the same stress response that would be triggered under a real threat. Try it and then take a minute to stretch, breathe, and stay quiet. You just can't be that stressed when you do. So, again, be big and breathe.

The first half of this book has been about how we've evolved and how we tick. We now have an idea why we have stress and why we need it. It's not the big, bad devil it's portrayed to be. It's there to fire us up and give us direction. There is always a fork in the stress road and it's up to us to make sure we go down the one that helps us get shit done and makes things better. The other road only has grief and ulcers and will make you walk around, head down, kicking stones. We now understand the concepts of New Brain and Old Brain and where our stress is generated. Remember that most of the bad stress we feel originates from either fear or disappointment, and integrating your New Brain to solve problems rather than create them will get you along the road to attaining *eudemonia*.

Now that we have done the groundwork, it's time to explore Section II and become *Stress Teflon*.

SECTION II

WHAT YOU NEED TO BECOME STRESS TEFLON

– C H A P T E R   7 –

THE GREEKS WORKED IT OUT YEARS AGO

'Happiness depends upon ourselves.'

—Aristotle

What is eudemonia, really?

The Greek philosopher Epicurus lived in the 300s BC. He was born on a beautiful Greek island, where he spent his youth learning the traditional philosophy of the Greek masters. He found, however, that much of what he was learning he either didn't particularly agree with or found uninteresting or irrelevant. By the time he was in his twenties, he decided to go it alone, forget about what he had been taught, and develop his own philosophy. Whilst Greek philosophy tackled lofty issues like the meaning of life or the nature of the universe, Epicurus decided to apply the tools of philosophy to the simpler issue of how to live a happy life.

He concluded that pleasure was the goal of a happy life, and he set up a school to both live and teach his new ideas. Almost immediately the 'real' philosophers came to associate Epicurus, his philosophy, and his school with self-indulgence and extravagance. Rumours started to circulate that life at the Garden (the name of his live-in school) was all feasts, drunkenness, and casual sex, and it's those associations with the word epicurean that persist even today. But life at the Garden was less like the Las Vegas strip and more like a hippy commune. You see, whilst people tend to jump to certain conclusions as soon as the word 'pleasure' is mentioned, Epicurus applied rational analysis (the great tool of philosophy) to first determine what it is that makes life pleasurable before jumping into the pursuit of pleasure. The answer to this turned out not to be the usual assumptions of a big house, gourmet food, and lots of stuff. Epicurus decided that to enjoy a happy life filled with pleasure you really only require three things beyond your basic survival needs: friendship, freedom, and thought.

Friendship, freedom, and thought. It sounds like Epicurus knew how to objectively flourish. These three things look a lot like what we have been talking about. Friendship is pretty straightforward. It's about social bonds. You need people you care about and who care about you. You need people who respect you for whom you are and couldn't care less what kind of car you drive, people you feel close to and with whom you can share your experiences.

Freedom is about pride. Epicurus and his friends didn't want to be trapped in jobs or lifestyles, doing things they had to do. It's not that they didn't want to work; it's that they wanted to spend their time doing things that were meaningful to them, things that made them feel proud rather than things that were either meaningless, or worse, not very nice, just to earn the money to pay for that house they didn't really need.

Thought is about using your rational New Brain to manage the fears and anxieties that the emotional Old Brain can't help throwing up at you.

Now, it should be noted that Epicurus wasn't saying that you can't have all the other stuff and be happy. The point is that friendship, freedom, and thought are paramount. If nothing gets in the way of those, then you should be fine. If you can have friendship, freedom, and thought, you will be happy. If you also have a nice house, enjoy fun holidays, and appreciate good food, then go you. It's just that we naturally seem to focus on the latter to provide happiness and barely give the former a thought.

The Greeks do rock.

So, our goal here is to objectively flourish, to embrace the good stress and let the bad stress simply slide off. By understanding Cronk, stealing some ideas from ancient Greece, and adding a modern twist, we have the foundations of *Stress Teflon*: security of a tribe, pride through contribution, and honest self-awareness.

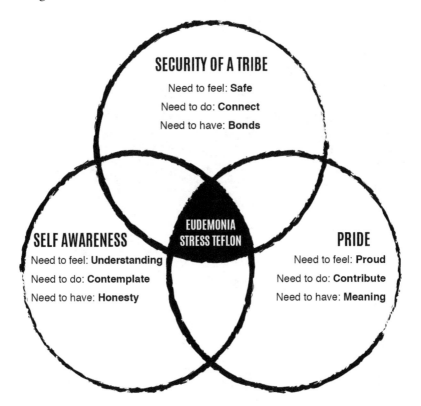

THE THREE FOUNDATIONS OF STRESS TEFLON

The three rings here show us the overlap that we need to achieve *eudemonia* and become *Stress Teflon*. In short, we need to feel secure with the people around us, we need to feel pride through making a contribution, and we need honest self-awareness. When these three needs are met, we are in the golden zone for both achieving *eudemonia* and becoming *Stress Teflon*. The following chapters will investigate these needs and give us a few examples of how to fulfil them.

– C H A P T E R 8 –

IT'S A TRIBAL THING

'The only way to have a true friend is to be one.'

—Ralph Waldo Emerson

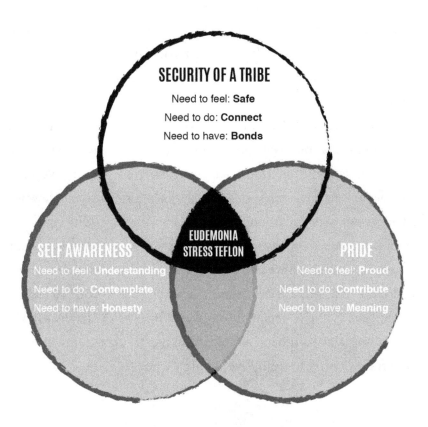

SECURITY OF A TRIBE

Need to feel: **Safe**

Need to do: **Connect**

Need to have: **Bonds**

SELF AWARENESS

Need to feel: **Understanding**

Need to do: **Contemplate**

Need to have: **Honesty**

EUDEMONIA
STRESS TEFLON

PRIDE

Need to feel: **Proud**

Need to do: **Contribute**

Need to have: **Meaning**

FOUNDATION ONE: SECURITY

To feel safe, we must connect with people and maintain and create the bonds that will strengthen our tribe.

We forget it sometimes, but we're pack animals. Like Cronk, we need to belong because if we don't, if we are rejected by our tribe, our chances of survival drop dramatically. And what's more stressful than a looming, painful death? Humans are communal by nature. We need the support of our tribe, or pack, to feel safe, loved, and purposeful. And we need to contribute in a way that makes us feel good about being ourselves. We're not solitary creatures like, say, a wolverine, which prefers a life alone. Maybe that's why Wolverine is such a miserable character out there in comic book land. Let's be honest, aside from Hugh Jackman's six-pack and the cool claws, no one wants to be Wolverine. We need a pack, and we need to feel that we happily belong to it.

The response I had to the news of Ragsy's diagnosis, that powerful inclination to help people in need, particularly when they're close to us, is born from our innate dedication to tribalism. Working together as a tribe has made us humans what we are today. It's how we establish our sense of belonging and personal safety. Our collective set of knowledge, communicated from person to person, generation to generation, is how we learn, innovate, and adapt at such acceler-ated rates. Without a tribe, humans, by nature, are prone to feeling lonely, fearful, and generally incomplete. Once we've established our need to be part of a tribe, it almost consumes us, becoming our most important priority in nearly everything we do.

THE PAIN OF SOCIAL REJECTION

In the early 2000s, scientists Naomi Eisenberger and Matthew Lieberman at the University of California Los Angeles (UCLA) and Kipling Williams at Purdue University found that social rejection activates many of the same brain regions involved in physical pain.[12] Pain, in case you didn't know, is designed to stop you from doing something that will harm you. Without pain, you might leave your hand on an oven hotplate or walk around on a broken leg. Pain stops you from doing things that aren't beneficial. Sounds like evolution 101, right?

The scientists wanted to look at the relationship between social rejection and pain. They set up a game called Cyberball, in which three online players throw a virtual ball to each other. They placed a subject in an fMRI scanner that can map activity inside the brain. As the game continued, the other two players began to exclude the subject and eventually he was never thrown the ball.

The rejected person's fMRI immediately showed increased activity in the pain centres of the brain (the dorsal anterior cingulate and the anterior insula, if you want to nerd out on me). This was a game of no importance. It was an experiment that involved throwing a virtual ball. Yet the brain's pain centres lit up like a Christmas tree when the subject was left out. Pain is a form of stress, and being excluded increases stress tenfold.

In Cronk's time, being cast out of the tribe was a death sentence. Everything wanted to kill you back then and we needed people around us to be safe. It kind of makes sense then that social rejection will stimulate the pain centres in the brain and stop you doing the

---

12 Naomi L. Eisenberger, Matthew D. Lieberman, Kipling D. Williams, 'Does rejection hurt? An fMRI study of social exclusion', *Science* 302, no. 5643 (10 October 2003): 290–292.

things that may cause rejection. In short, evolution stops you from being an arsehole and getting kicked out of the tribe. If it hurts, you stop doing it.

I'm not sure if your conscience is a social thing or an evolutionary thing, but it might explain why you feel guilty if you do something you know is wrong, no matter how small—the knot in the stomach that occurs if you lie to a friend about why you can't come to her daughter's ballet recital, for instance, or the shame you feel for cheating at a game or for eating all the ice cream. Could it be that we have evolved to be nice to ensure we avoid the pain of being kicked out of the tribe?

Think of it another way. Your narcissistic, arsehole boss, who has no social skills and only cares about himself, just isn't as evolved as you.

SARAH'S STORY

Teenage girls are the queens of exclusion. All fourteen-year-old girls know they have the power to hurt by excluding others.

Sarah is your average, fourteen-year-old girl. She's fun, she loves sports, she's healthy, she does well at school, and she tries really hard to please people. She loves her parents, has lots of great friends, and has a group of five or six friends that she's super tight with. But lately, she's been going through that stage that all fourteen-year-olds go through as they mature. All of a sudden she started getting really tired all the time, and she stays in bed far more than she used to. She doesn't really want to talk to her parents, and she's not the same motivated kid she once was. As Sarah's attitude and health change so dramatically, her parents wonder what the hell has happened to this kid. Is this normal or has something happened?

It turns out something has happened. A rumour has been going around school that Sarah sent a boy on Facebook a nude picture of herself, and all of her friends have ostracized her because of it. Sarah no longer feels that she belongs to her tribe and it's made her stress levels increase, which has made her sick.

What we know now is that the part of the brain that lights up when you get kicked out of your tribe is exactly the same part of the brain that lights up if you break a leg. Why? Well, first the tribal reason.

In Cronk's time, if you got kicked out of your group, you were fucked. You were not going to find food as easily, if at all. Even if you did, you would likely be eaten by a predator before long because you had no one to protect you.

Tribalism, or community, is biologically ingrained in us, so much so that even today we have a strong urge to do things that make us stay part of the tribe. We have to look after people, adhere to customs and rules, and basically just not be an arsehole. If you're an arsehole, you're going to get kicked out of the tribe, right? And if you got kicked out of the tribe in 10,000 BC, you were fucked.

Everything our brain does is designed to protect us. If you break your leg, it hurts when you step on your leg. So you don't step on your leg. And that exact same part of your brain that stops you stepping on your leg when your leg is broken is the same part of your brain that will fire up if you get kicked out of your social group. In Cronk's time it was 100 per cent about survival. In Sarah's time it's 100 per cent about feeling she belongs to her group because if she doesn't, the stress is going to be debilitating, just like in Cyberball.

Tribes like Cronk's are almost unrecognizable compared to tribes today. Our tribal instincts around them, however, are still the same.

We certainly have more tribes to choose from today, and a kind of tribal tier system has developed because of it. Chances are that if you've ever spent time traveling abroad, you've met people displaying their support for your local sports team, university, business, and so on, or maybe you caught their accent or overheard their conversation and determined that you shared a common place of origin with them. You might have even struck up a curious conversation with them to find out for sure. That conversation usually goes something like this: 'Hey, go [insert team name]. Are you from [insert region or city name]?' If they are from your city or region, then you're off to the races as the tribal breakdown begins, ticking off a mental checklist intended to see how closely connected the two of you are: 'What part of [insert region or city name] are you from? Where did you go to high school? Wait, what's your name? Do you know so and so? How about so and so?' At worst, you discover that the stranger is just another stranger, but if all tiers check out, you might have discovered a long-lost relative.

What are we doing when this happens? What's the point of breaking down the degrees of relation with a stranger? It's an instinctual line of questioning to help feel connected to someone when we're feeling out of place or alone. We have a primal need to assemble a tribe when we feel threatened, and the closer we feel to someone—from supporting the same sports team to being a blood relative—the safer we feel including them.

That type of tribal checklist affects us in all sorts of ways we might not expect, everything from whom we marry to where we live to our well-being and even the physical shape of our brain. That's right, even our brain size has been influenced by what researchers call the sizing up effect. A 2016 Cardiff University study found that 'humans have evolved a disproportionately large brain as a result of sizing each other up in large cooperative social groups.'[13]

We desperately want to find our tribe in an increasingly interconnected world of tribes, and once we do, we instinctively take great pride in caring for it. Why? I think it links back to achieving *eudemonia*. Caring about your tribe and showing that you care are, Aristotle believed, primal instincts for us all. By committing ourselves to 'activity in accordance with virtue', the Greek philosopher believed we would reach a state of personal bliss, which we are all instinctively trying to find. What defines an activity in accordance with virtue? Well, scholars go back and forth on defining it exactly, as what is right to one person may not be right to another, but at its core is the idea that we all have the innate potential to live a life filled with happiness and well-being simply by doing what is morally right, which ultimately helps our tribe to flourish. And if our tribe flourishes, so do we.

Think of it another way. Your parents, teachers or coaches likely warned you that if you didn't perform as well as others at school, at work, or at a particular sport, you would not succeed. What we're telling kids underneath it all is that they have to be successful in the eyes of their tribe, or else their life is going to be terrible. Failure is stressful. Failing simply means that a person isn't as good as the rest of the tribe and should be banished in some way or another because of it—for example, kicked off the team, fired from the job, held back a grade, which can be stress factor warp ten.

We may think of these warnings as just fairly innocuous comments, but they carry a long-term mentality well into adulthood:

---

13   Science Daily, 'Large human brain evolved as a result of "sizing each other up"', 12 August 2016, https://www.sciencedaily.com/releases/2016/08/160812074537. htm.

'You have to work hard. You have to get this. You have to do that. You have to dress this certain way otherwise the kids at school are going to bully you . . .' The desire to conform all comes back to our primal need to survive and avoid the stress of exclusion.

We may also look at how nice the lives of celebrities or the super wealthy look from the outside, with their possessions, looks, or talents that the tribe admires, and feel that without those things, we matter less to the tribe or perhaps don't belong at all.

The author and lecturer Alain de Botton refers to our fear of failure as more of a fear of being ostracized. He calls that phenomenon of comparing ourselves to the most admired members of our tribe status anxiety, a condition afflicting members of tribes that ascribe respect and love according to social hierarchy. Status anxiety helps fuel the drive to do better at work, at school, in the game, at home, in the community, and so on, because it helps us feel more certain about our position in the world. Our status anxiety is really a symptom of our fear of not fitting in with our tribe, more than anything else. After all, if we *don't* fit in with the tribe, our primal instincts tell us that our survival is in jeopardy. But before you bend over backwards trying to gain the acceptance of a particular tribe, you should really consider what the tribe does to make you happy. Does it really matter to you if you have the biggest house, the nicest car, or the latest cell phone? Is this even the tribe you really want to be part of?

In Cronk's case, he got just as much in return from his tribe for his efforts to contribute to it. Because he was an excellent hunter, he would lead the charge when he and his tribe mates went out hunting. He killed a tiger, a feat held in high esteem to his tribe, and he regularly brought home the biggest hunks of meat to feed his tribe. And for his accomplishments, Cronk was regarded as the top dog, the alpha of his pack. He got the best pieces of meat from his kills, the cosiest bed perhaps, the best mate, the best hunting tools, and more.

Later on, when he couldn't hunt as well as he had in his younger days, he contributed to the tribe by spending his time teaching the children and building up other people. That was his way of providing for the tribe he loved and helping to ensure its survival. Cronk was gaining plenty in return, of course: the safety of being part of a community and the pride of being well respected by his peers.

Before vast empires reigned, before the glow of television came flashing across every living room, before the dawn of the digital society, tribes like Cronk's were smaller, tighter, less concerned with the individual. A tribe like Cronk's might have only totalled fifty to a hundred members. Now, as technology continues to connect us, for better and for worse, our tribe is seemingly infinite. Take Facebook for example. The social media site intends to connect you to your friends, your tribe. Keeping in mind that the average Facebook user today has 338 friends[14] and a steady stream of insights into the lives

of billions all over the world, the average person's virtual tribe is much larger than our primal instincts are accustomed to. Is it possible to *really* be friends with 338 people, to be invested in their lives, to speak or visit with them on a regular basis? No. In fact, the evolutionary psychologist Robin Dunbar spent more than a decade researching the capacity for human relationships and determined that, on average,

14   Steven Mazie, 'Do you have too many Facebook friends?', Big Think, http://bigthink.com/praxis/do-you-have-too-many-facebook-friends.

we cannot maintain more than 150 relationships. From military units to communes to corporations, once a group reaches 150 members, it usually splits apart in some way. Some fracture into smaller groups, some open additional offices elsewhere but stay unified, and some disband altogether.

TRIBES WITHIN THE TRIBE

Modern tribes can take many forms, too. Take my mate Kevin, for example, who found his tribe in a way that isn't exactly virtual but isn't quite real either.

Kevin and I have known each other for more than thirty years, and by sheer serendipity, he managed to marry one of my best friends. But there's something you have to understand about Kev. He loves *Star Wars*. I don't mean that he likes the movies a lot. I mean he literally loves everything about them. Everything. He also loves *Star Trek* (don't confuse the two; it really pisses fans off), but it's in *Star Wars*, and in particular, the dark side, where Kev truly found his tribe.

You see, Kev is a Sith lord. For six years he has been the commanding officer of the Queensland 501st Legion. If you are like me, you may not know a lot about *Star Wars*. I saw the first one in 1977 and punished myself by watching Jar Jar Binks when one of the movies featuring him first came out. (I don't remember which episode.) Obviously, I'm not a big fan of *Star Wars*, despite people constantly telling me, '*Luke*, I am your father.' Apparently, my father—and yours too—is Darth Vader, and in the 501st Legion, Kev is Darth Vader.

Kev is a bit over six feet tall and in his Darth Vader costume, he looks very imposing. The black outfit is complete with big boots and a heavy breastplate that contains a voice-altering box that makes any words Kev utters sound exactly like James Earl Jones, the voice of Vader in the movies. It's pretty impressive. As the Sith lord, Kev organises a group of 150 *Star Wars* fans who do some amazing work in our community.

They visit children's hospitals. They raise money for great causes, like the Starlight Foundation. And they bring a lot of joy to millions of *Star Wars* fans. When Vader and his stormtroopers enter a hospital, the kids forget their illnesses and they are transported to a galaxy far, far away.

'It feels great to walk into a hospital and feel like you've made someone's day', Kev explained when talking about his work with the 501st. 'It takes up a lot of time, and it's easy to spend a lot of money with this hobby . . . [but] it's great to have a hobby you love that also does a huge amount of good', Kev said. His Vader costume alone cost more than $7,000. It has the voice box, ice pockets (it's hot in that suit in Queensland), and an awesome helmet. Couple this with the cost of travel to conferences like Comic-Con and Supanova and you can see just how committed he and his group are to the dark side.

What draws people to the 501st Legion? According to Kev, it's the sense of belonging and the desire to immerse himself in another word that allows him to park the demands of modern life for a while. Putting on a stormtrooper outfit is quite liberating for him. He has anonymity, a sense of belonging, and the pride that comes along with doing good things for charity.

The 501st Legion has brought together over eleven thousand people for a common love, and because of it, it has facilitated marriages and provided a place where people feel safe. Safety and acceptance are key to any tribe. That sense of safety has seen gay stormtroopers come out to the members of the 501st before they even told their families. 'Being gay is nowhere near as bad as being a Jedi', one gay stormtrooper joked. Having a common love is a great way to build a tribe. Whether it's *Star Wars*, crochet, or stamp collecting, a common love is a way to gain acceptance, just as it was in Cronk's time. The need to belong is a really strong human survival tool. Having that sense of belonging will make you more resilient and decrease harmful stress.

– CHAPTER 9 –

CONTRIBUTION AND THE NEED TO FEEL VALUED

'Happiness lies in the joy of achievement and the thrill of creative effort.'

—Franklin D. Roosevelt

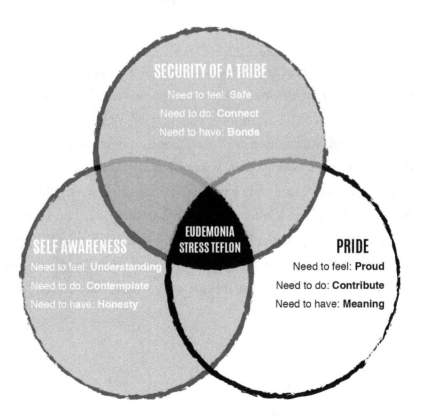

FOUNDATION TWO: PRIDE AND CONTRIBUTION

To feel proud of ourselves, we must contribute to the world and have meaning in our life.

Cronk felt an innate need to contribute to his tribe. The warm, fuzzy feeling of pride that went along with it made him and his mates feel valued and kept their tribe together. In other words, staying together kept them feeling safe and happy.

Not much has changed. We still need to contribute to feel good and have well-being. Genuine self-confidence is essential for *eudemonia* and a big part of making ourselves *Stress Teflon*. Remember that the biggest cause of toxic stress is the fear you can't handle a given situation. Clear memories of occasions when you handled a difficult situation are where self-confidence is born. 'I have been through something like this before and I sorted it out then. I can sort it out now!' That's how you get *eudemonia*, objective flourishing and the belief in yourself that comes from actions, from contributing. True belief is born from actions and achieving something. Do something! Help someone, contribute, and be part of your tribe.

Pride and contribution are linked to the production of serotonin that we discussed in chapter 5. If you look at the diagram with our three circles, we can see what happens when we don't have *pride from inside*. Being safe and self-aware are important needs but without doing something positive, you never quite attain *eudemonia*. To get happiness and to objectively flourish, you need to *do something*! You need pride in yourself, and that pride comes from your actions, not your words or thoughts.

WHAT HAPPENS IF YOU LACK PRIDE FROM INSIDE?

Because serotonin is a mood balancer, those with a chronic deficiency typically experience intense bouts of melancholy and depression. The more serotonin there is in the system, the more pride you feel in yourself. A large percentage of people with depression get an enormous amount of benefit from taking medication to help them feel happier. The most commonly prescribed antidepressants are SSRIs, drugs designed to keep serotonin in your system longer.

BRAIN BOX

SSRIs

Selective serotonin reuptake inhibitors (SSRIs) are the most commonly prescribed type of antidepressant. SSRIs ease depression by increasing levels of serotonin in the brain. Serotonin is one of the chemical messengers (neurotransmitters) that carry signals between brain cells. SSRIs block the reabsorption (reuptake) of serotonin in the brain, making more serotonin available for longer periods. SSRIs are called selective because they seem to primarily affect serotonin, not other neurotransmitters. SSRIs also may be used to treat conditions other than depression, such as anxiety disorders. Common branded SSRIs are Prozac, Zoloft, and Lexapro.

Several years ago, I was having a regular check-up with my doctor and happened to mention I was feeling a bit flat, not quite myself. Business was fantastic, my wife and daughter were both great, but I wasn't feeling my usual upbeat, happy self.

My doctor quickly reached for the prescription pad and wrote out a script for Lexapro. I trust doctors and knew he had my best interest at heart. I got the pills and started taking one a day. Within a week or two, I felt I had a lot more energy and was excited about the things I'd do again.

Just to be safe, though, I decided to do some Google doctoring (usually a bad idea) to find out a bit more about these tablets. This was three or four years ago, and at the time, I had never heard of serotonin. It's great stuff, I learned.

Serotonin feels wonderful, and these tablets were making me feel like my usual self, but something was nagging in the back of my mind. I am an eternal optimist. Friends say I live in Luke-land, a place where everyone is nice, things always turn out for the best, and everyone does the right thing. If I live in Luke land, why do I need to take an antidepressant? I decided, with the help of my doctor, to wean myself off the tablets—I had only been on them a month—and concentrate on *doing things* that make more serotonin. I started by looking for reasons to be grateful, which led me to help more people at work get better at their jobs. You might say that I started putting my heart and soul into things again. You have to care and show you care to produce serotonin. When you do that, you will produce more serotonin and the *pride from inside* will help you feel good about yourself (an essential part of being *Stress Teflon*).

Depression affects 350 million people worldwide. In the USA, in 2012, one in every twelve young people between the ages of eighteen and twenty-two reported a major depressive episode in the previous year.[15] Depression would be awful! I'm not a doctor, but you have to wonder how many people, like me, have wrongly been prescribed these tablets by well-meaning GPs.

Sadness and grief are normal human emotions. We all have those feelings from time to time, but they usually go away within a few days. Major depression is something more. It's a period of overwhelming sadness. It involves a loss of interest in things that used to bring pleasure. Those feelings are usually accompanied by other emotional and physical symptoms.

'If it can be solved by $5,000 or a new boyfriend, it's not depression.'

—Ned Shorter, Hannah Professor of History of Medicine and Professor of Psychiatry, University of Toronto

Being told you have depression could well be a self-fulfilling prophecy, sending your New Brain into overdrive and creating a feedback loop of worry. If you are on antidepressants, talk to your doctor and together look for ways to find positivity in your life. Doctors are trying to help, and in a lot of situations, Prozac may well be the best answer, but my feeling is doctors are reaching for the Rx pad a bit too quickly.

When researching depression for this book, I discovered that the demographic with the highest rate of depression was women aged forty to fifty-nine, with approximately one in eight women diagnosed with depression.

---

15   Ann Pietrangelo, 'Depression and mental health by the numbers: facts, statistics, and you', Healthline, http://www.healthline.com/health/depression/facts-statistics-infographic#2.

This statistic really concerns me. Most of the women I care about are in this demographic, which means that I likely know a few who are dealing with depression.

I decided to look into why so many fantastic women become depressed with the onset of middle age. I conducted a little impromptu survey. The responses ranged from 'past a certain age, women feel invisible' to 'I feel like I'm not needed or appreciated anymore.'

From the moment little boys are toddlers, we tell them they are strong, and we tell girls they are beautiful. Being beautiful, therefore, is (wrongly) engrained in women as a measure of their worth. Botox, wrinkle creams, and bolt-on boobs have become million-dollar industries and are all part of the business of staying beautiful. Time waits for no one—except Christie Brinkley—and we are all going to get older. For many women, their departing youth also signals a departure in pride and self-worth.

'Enjoy the power and beauty of your youth. Oh, never mind. You will not understand the power and beauty of your youth until they've faded. But trust me, in twenty years you'll look back at photos of yourself and recall in a way you can't grasp now how much possibility lay before you and how fabulous you really looked.'

—Mary Schmidt, *Chicago Tribune*, 1 June 1997

Being a mother is a demanding job. You put your former priorities on hold to welcome into the world a demanding, pooping, vomiting bundle of joy. So much of a mum's day goes into looking after others. There are fantastic milestones, first steps, starting school, and all along the way, mums are there to help and nurture their child. Being a mum is the most overworked, underpaid job there is, but being a mum can also be the most rewarding job in the world.

When we look at stress, having a child tops the list for both good and bad stress. If you were trying to avoid stress, would you ever have a kid? No fucking way. The little bastards are a constant source of grief. But here's the deal: ask any parents what the best day of their life was and the answer is almost exclusively the day their kid was born. Mums understand the importance of their job and they take it really seriously.

It doesn't matter if you are a full-time mum or the CEO of a multinational company. The role of being a parent will be a very important part of your life and, at least in part, define your opinion of yourself. Whether you like it or not, how well you do in your role as a parent will have a big impact on how much *pride from inside* you experience. With serotonin being a major factor in well-being and mood, it makes sense that mums are susceptible to big fluctuations in happiness. My sister expresses it this way: 'Mums can only be as happy as their unhappiest child.' That is putting a lot of your well-being in the hands of others.

So why are so many women in their forties and fifties lacking the *pride from inside* and falling into the black hole of depression? To investigate this phenomenon, we are going to look back at the last decades of two women in this age group.

MICHELLE

Michelle and Jason met at university and fell in love instantly. They were both young and beautiful and ready to change the world. She finished her environmental science degree and started work with a not-for-profit that was dedicated to removing plastics from the ocean. Jason's law degree, along with a bit of help from his dad, secured him a great job at a big local firm and the five-year plan to become a partner was underway.

The two married and the kids followed soon after. For Michelle, saving the world would have to wait. She had two kids under two and her environmental impact didn't even get as far as boycotting disposable nappies. Jason made partner and the four of them moved into the nice house near good schools. Things were going great. She looked after the kids, made healthy lunches, helped with the school's swim team, and volunteered at the tuck shop on Thursdays. Her sense of self-worth came from serving others. She was a great mum, the kids loved her, and she never put herself first. That would be selfish.

Jason was really busy at work and rarely got home in time to eat with her and the kids. Business was going great, and although time was scarce, he always managed golf on Saturdays. Life for Jason and Michelle was going according to plan.

Fast forward fifteen years and Jason is senior partner, playing corporate golf days, and the family has moved into a bigger house near better schools. The kids are about to leave school, and like most teenagers, they only communicate with Mum via grunts and requests for money. They have their own car now, so Mum's taxi services aren't needed anymore.

Michelle's days are filled with housework and the occasional trip to the gym or the beauty salon. At forty, the greys are coming faster and Botox appears to be the only way to maintain the beauty of her youth. She can't move the muscles in her face anymore, but at least she doesn't have wrinkles. Getting a job is an option, but her degree is next to useless now and who would want to hire someone who hasn't worked for over a decade? She doesn't need the money, so why should she go through the stress and anxiety of learning new skills and trying to get a job? She would be starting at the bottom, too.

She has tried to talk Jason into a romantic trip to Italy, but he's not interested. Between work, golf, and his mates, Jason's life is pretty full. Michelle has put all her time into looking after the kids and Jason found joy elsewhere. Their relationship is now one of convenience rather than one of shared interests, mutual respect, and affection. It all hit home recently at her fortieth birthday. Jason's speech was not one filled with love and affection for his wife. It was more the type of speech the senior partner would give to a staff member. He actually said that 'her best work was ahead of her.'

Michelle was becoming the one in eight people in her demographic with depression. She found it hard to get excited about the things she used to love doing. She was putting on weight and the more she looked at her life, the fatter and sadder she got. The big house and the Mercedes were not doing it for her anymore.

If you have everything, and you are still sad, having everything just makes the depression worse. Understanding serotonin, choosing to be happy, and changing your outlook may be another option to consider.

The Harvard positive psychology author Shawn Achor outlines a twenty-one-day happiness advantage program. For twenty-one days, you need to journal three things you are grateful for and perform one act of kindness. My staff did this and they e-mailed me every day for twenty-one days. The journey was amazing! To start with, responses were on the lines of 'I'm grateful for Nutella and sunny days.' After a week or so, people began to really look for positives in their lives and the acts of kindness were fantastic.

My favourite act of kindness was when Jasmine put a post-it on the back of the toilet door in the public bathroom. She wrote the words 'You're beautiful!' on it. When she went back later, someone had written, 'So are you.' The message was right: they are both beautiful women and both had the *pride from inside* that comes from doing something nice.

JEN

Jenny Alcorn is a fifty-six-year-old former world duathlon (running and cycling) champion. Every morning she gets up, usually before dawn, and meets up to train and coach members of her Surfers Paradise Triathlon Club (SPTC). She has a body hardened from years of swimming, cycling, and running. She has muscular thighs from years on the bike, six-pack abs of steel, and wiry arms that would make me think twice about an arm wrestle. Her blonde hair (now more platinum) bounces behind her as she runs along the beachfront. Jenny loves her life. She loves training. She loves her role of developing promising juniors to become future champions. She even loves watching MAMILs (middle-aged men in Lycra) like me achieve their goals of dropping a few kilos. Jenny is one very content, rounded, beautiful, and happy human.

Always an athlete, Jenny started her sporting career as a hockey player. Her father was on the Australian hockey team, and she spent her weekends at the hockey field with a cut-down hockey stick, honing her skills. By the time she was old enough to join a team, she already had the skills and the fitness to excel at her chosen sport. She quickly made the state team as a junior and always enjoyed the bonds that exist from being part of a team.

When I asked Jenny if she was a star at hockey, her answer was a typical Jenny one: 'I wasn't fantastic, but I was always good at setting up for other people.' Jenny is a team player.

In her early twenties, she was on the verge of making the national team. She was very young and, by her own admission, didn't handle the stress of being at the pinnacle of the sport. She went back to her state team where, once again, she was confident, competent, and the glue that kept her team together. She was the team masseuse and, if I know Jen, looked after everyone.

Some friends from the gym convinced her to start cycling and then swimming, and before she knew it, she was doing triathlons. Pretty soon Jen had turned into an elite triathlete. She was the female winner of the ITU Duathlon World Championships in 1992 and spent a lot of the early '90s travelling the world as a professional athlete.

When competing as a professional was no longer an option, she started the Surfers Paradise Triathlon Club (SPTC). Since starting SPTC, Jen has trained champion triathletes like Olympians Emma

Snowsil (2008 gold medallist) and Ashleigh Gentle and has helped countless others achieve their triathlon and fitness goals.

In 2014 she decided to embark on a massive challenge. Together with six other members of the SPTC, she decided to climb Everest. They were going to compete in an Ironman triathlon. These gruelling events are held all over the world and consist of a 3.8-kilometre swim and a 180-kilometre cycle, followed by a full marathon (forty-two kilometres). The goal of anyone who does an Ironman is to get to Kona in Hawaii. To triathletes, Kona is like Wimbledon or the Olympics. It's the ultimate. To get invited to Kona, you must place in the top two of a qualifying Ironman event.

Jen and her SPTC teammates set their Ironman sights on Busselton, the sleepy seaside town three hours south of Perth. She did the work, sorted out all the nutrition for the race, and had a game plan in her head.

She started the swim on the far left of the pack and had clear water all the way to the turn. After finishing the swim, she made a quick transition onto the bike and was away. The fluctuating winds made the cycle difficult, but she was still on track. Toward the end of the cycle, she started to get some pains in her feet. Coming off the bike and starting the run, she was in agony. She willed herself to keep going. About five kilometres in, she stopped for a bathroom break, quickly took off her shoes, and gave her feet a massage. This got the blood flowing and her feet were good to go again. As the run continued, she passed several of the boys from SPTC. Some of them were really struggling. Despite having been on the road for over nine hours, Jen still mustered up the energy to give them a pep talk and some encouragement.

Ten and a half hours after starting the race with the swim, Jenny crossed the finish line. She was an Ironman. Completely spent, she celebrated with the joy that comes from a job well done. She won her age group by over forty minutes, which also placed her among the top three competitors in age groups fifteen years younger. She was going to Kona!

The Kona training had some injury hiccups, but she was back on track until July 2015. After doing a hundred-kilometre ride with her Sunday morning squad, Jen decided to do an extra twenty kilometres on her own. She was practising getting down on her profile bars. The profile bars make a cyclist more aerodynamic but they sacrifice an element of control. Riders generally only use their profile bars when the road is straight and there is no need for breaking. In an Ironman event it is vital to have nutrition and hydration needs planned out. Jen, while putting food into a back pocket, lost some of her usual concentration. She swerved to miss a block of wood on the road, lost control of the bike, and crashed into the back of a stationary SUV. She was doing thirty-five kilometres an hour.

Numerous X-rays and MRIs confirmed what she already knew. She was busted up! Three broken ribs, a fractured collarbone, a wrist broken in three places, and a few broken fingers. With ten weeks to go, it seemed her Kona dream was over.

Two days later, though, Jen borrowed a recumbent stationary bike, parked it in front of the TV, and did several hours a day in a vain attempt to keep her dream alive. Fortunately, sanity prevailed and after listening to doctors and her friends, she officially pulled out of the big race.

A horrific injury like this, particularly to an elite athlete, can often cause a spiral into depression. This didn't happen to Jen even though she was in her fifties and knew the time was running out to achieve another dream. Why was Jen so resilient and able to cope so well with this terrible setback?

I believe Jen's ability to cope with her setback can be credited to her social reward system and the caveman yearning to be part of the tribe. Although the triathlon is an individual sport, most of the training is done in larger groups.

Let's look at our caveman reward system for triathlon training. All training sessions have a goal in mind. You swim a certain number of laps, ride to the top of a particular hill, or run a certain number of Ks. All of these goals elicit a drive-to-thrive (dopamine) response that keeps you going until you get to the finish line. Endorphins help mask your physical pain while dopamine helps you stay focused on achieving your goal.

It feels great to rest your legs after a training session and most of that sense of satisfaction comes from the natural release of dopamine. If all these endorphins and dopamine feel so wonderful, why is it that it always feels better to train in a group?

The answer is your pride-from-inside chemical, serotonin. Serotonin is what makes you keep going when your legs feel like jelly. Pride in yourself is a great feeling, but that is not where serotonin ends. The extraordinary thing about serotonin is that you get the *exact same reward* from witnessing people in your tribe achieving *their* goals. It is this cumulative release of chemicals that is responsible for the power of group training.

Jen is the coach, strategist, and motivator for the entire SPTC group. The fact that she was now injured was disappointing, but it didn't have the devastating effect that often occurs when elite athletes have their dreams shattered.

For most athletes, their sporting prowess is what provides their sense of self-worth. They feel pride in themselves based predominantly on their ability to excel in their chosen sport. For Jen, her exceptional ability as a triathlete is only a small part of where her sense of self-worth and pride come from. A large percentage of her serotonin (pride) comes from watching her squad members achieve *their goals*. She has a big part to play in other people's success, and it is this sense of contribution that kept Jen positive when she was unable to train and to fulfil her dream.

Twelve months after the disappointment of her 2015 crash, Jen got another chance to compete at Kona. In true Jenny Alcorn spirit, she ground out another win and at the age of fifty-seven she was once again a world champion. Her entire tribe was elated.

Jen is objectively flourishing because she has *eudemonia*. She is *Stress Teflon*. Fortunately, you don't have to do anything as ridiculously crazy as an Ironman to get the same feelings. Find new ways to contribute, find new ways to be a bigger part of your tribe, and *do* something that gives you *pride from inside*. Helping other people and doing something selfless will help.

I'll give you another example. My big sister Jenni has five degrees, is a university lecturer, and is a really smart and overall brave woman. At the age of forty-eight, Jenni left her job as a teacher and decided to pursue a law degree. Imagine going into class and being the same age as everyone else's mum? She did it and she smashed it, graduating near the top of the class and eventually coming back to the university as a lecturer. I am massively proud of her achievements and often brag with great pride about how smart my big sister is. These things, however, don't really do it for Jenni. These sorts of achievements aren't where she gets her *pride from inside*.

A while ago she discovered an organisation called Orange Sky Laundry. Founded by two young guys in their early twenties, Orange Sky has a fleet of vans that are fitted out with washing machines and dryers and do laundry for homeless people. Jenni coordinates our local Orange Sky service and, with the help of over fifty volunteers, she gives dignity to people who are struggling. She doesn't get paid for it and is routinely up at 5 a.m. to collect *Bubbles* (the name of the laundry van) to do some washing for people who live on the margins of our society. How many people would go to work at 5 a.m. for free? Jenni does.

Andrew Tobias once said there was no such thing as true altruism. He may be right. She may not admit it, but the reason Jenni does it is biological. It feels good to help others and it feels good to make a positive difference in the world. Cronk and his ancestors survived because we have pride-from-inside carrots. They make us stick together and they make it feel good to help people in our tribe. Altruism is when we look after other people's welfare, without getting anything in return. Even though you want to help others, you always get something in return. Evolution and the need to be part of a tribe ensure that it feels good to do good things that make the tribe stronger.

For Jen, Jenni, and Cronk, just achieving their personal goals was not enough. They needed to know they had contributed to their team/tribe/pack/community—however you want to define it—to attain true joy from their efforts. And like them, if you are to achieve lasting happiness, pride, and well-being, you have to help others along the way. A journey travelled solely for yourself will, quite literally, only lead to misery.

I'm going to finish this chapter with one final thought.

Is the world a better place because you are in it? If the answer is no . . . think harder.

If it's still no, do something positive and contribute.

–CHAPTER 10–

A LOOK IN THE ROOM OF MIRRORS

'We know what we are but know not what we may be.'

—William Shakespeare

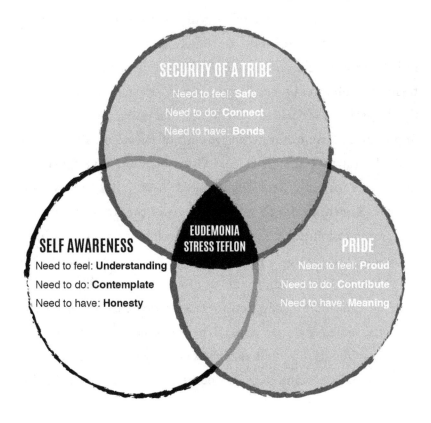

SECURITY OF A TRIBE
Need to feel: **Safe**
Need to do: **Connect**
Need to have: **Bonds**

EUDEMONIA
STRESS TEFLON

SELF AWARENESS
Need to feel: **Understanding**
Need to do: **Contemplate**
Need to have: **Honesty**

PRIDE
Need to feel: **Proud**
Need to do: **Contribute**
Need to have: **Meaning**

FOUNDATION THREE: HONEST SELF-AWARENESS

Use honest rational thoughts to improve your weaknesses, accept your faults, and develop an improvement mind-set.

PROGRESSTINATION

By now we know that integrating our two brains is important and that *eudemonia* can only be achieved by understanding what you are thinking and why you are thinking it and asking whether it is helping. This brings us to the final piece of the *Stress Teflon* puzzle: honest self-awareness.

Most of us are very familiar with how procrastination works. We've all put things off until a deadline draws close and panic sets in before we finally get them done. Whether studying for an exam, taking the rubbish out, or filing the report for your boss, we all know the dynamics of procrastination. We put off doing something that is important in favour of watching re-runs of *Friends* on TV or surfing YouTube for silly animal videos. Procrastination always makes us feel a little bit guilty and disappointed in ourselves, but we do it anyway. Sometimes it's an attempt to avoid the stress and pressure of our responsibilities, and sometimes it's simply that we'd rather do something else. So we do just that.

Now let me introduce you to procrastination's slightly better-looking, guilt-minimising cousin *progresstination*. Progresstination is doing something that appears to be positive, productive, and somewhat important, but in reality it's taking your time and attention off the *most* important goals. It doesn't come with procrastination's guilt and disappointment, because you are actually doing something positive.

Procrastinating has some stress associated with it and a small dint to the pride. No one has a desire to be lazy. You don't go to bed at night and think, *That was great. I'm really glad I sat on the couch and ate that box of cookies.* Because progresstinating involves doing positive things, we save ourselves the guilt trip and still feel okay about ourselves: 'Hey! At least I got the sock drawer sorted out. Now that I can get dressed faster, I'll accomplish loads more work—tomorrow.'

That's harmless enough, isn't it?

Well, if you want to plod through life and live a safe and easy existence, then yes, it's harmless enough. But if you're looking for *eudemonia* (objective flourishing from doing great things), this type of life often lacks passion and fulfilment and will eventually leave you feeling empty.

Progresstination, then, can be described as procrastination for your dreams. Like all human reward systems, dopamine (your drive-to-thrive hormone) gives you a little feel-good chemical hit every time you do something positive. The system ensures we continue to do things that are in our best interest. With progresstination, you get the feel-good hit just by ticking things off your to-do list. This list may be things that need to be done, but are they getting you any closer to your dream?

What if you have an inner drive to do something remarkable, something that will light a fire of contentment and self-satisfaction? My company uses the term BHAG (big hairy audacious goal).

I actually prefer BHAD, which, contrary to how it sounds, isn't a Baghdad kebab vendor. It means 'big hairy audacious dream.' By dream, I don't mean unachievable fantasy. It still needs to be realistic. But a dream is limitless, has no end point, and allows your imagination to run free. Martin Luther King's speech in Washington wouldn't have been as good if it had used the words 'I have a goal . . .'

Goals are important when you look at sales figures, weight loss, or grades in school. Goals fire up your drive-to-thrive (dopamine) reward systems, which are really effective in getting things done. The only problem is, as soon as we achieve them, we move the goal posts and need bigger sales targets or even better grades.

Dreams, on the other hand, combine both your personal and social reward systems. You need both to achieve balance.

Your BHAD is something that will make your world a better place and fire up your pride-from-inside (serotonin) rewards system. You don't even have to come up with your own BHAD. You can join a tribe and share theirs. Look at Jenni and Orange Sky Laundry. She bought into their dream of bringing dignity to homeless people. She did something positive, saw a need, and decided to contribute. To achieve your BHAD, you have to be conscious of progresstination.

I really wanted to write a book. I knew it would take a lot of research, so I researched and researched. Eventually, I'd done so much research that if I were to include everything I had learnt, the book would have looked like *War and Peace*. My research was a way of progresstinating and not actually *writing the book*. I lacked the belief that I could actually write an entire book. (I'm stoked you have got this far too.) This is an example of my not buying into my BHAD. Self-doubt causes progresstination and dreams don't get fulfilled.

Lacking self-belief is what makes you progresstinate. Sometimes your BHAD appears so big and daunting that you don't know where to start. Businesses all over the world have sales targets, but do they have dreams? Do they have employees who fully buy into those dreams?

The author Seth Godin coined a great term to describe something similar. He called it sheepwalking. Businesses, as you may know, are filled with sheepwalkers.

I'll let Seth define the term: 'I define "sheepwalking" as the outcome of hiring people who have been raised to be obedient and giving them a brain-dead job and enough fear to keep them in line.'

How many people are sheepwalking through their workday? Do you ever think that there must be a better way? Have you ever said, 'What if management did this?' If you have asked these questions of yourself and done nothing about them, you are sheepwalking and progresstinating.

How do we catch ourselves progresstinating? That's easy. Just look for the warning signs.

- You have no clear idea of what your BHAD is. What do you want?

- If you have a BHAD, you have no deadline for achieving it. Without a deadline, you never get a sense of urgency that fires you up to get shit done. Dreams need little goals and little deadlines along the way.

- You tell yourself why your idea *won't* work before it has a chance to get off the ground.

- You get easily distracted and only complete the small here-and-now tasks. Multitasking is a great way to keep progresstinating.

- You tick the easy-to-do tasks off the list while the bigger, harder tasks remain untouched.

- You have a fear of failure, or even scarier, a fear of success. Succeeding at your big dream will change the status quo and move you out of your comfort zone. Is that scary to you?

So how do we stop progresstinating? Well, the first step is to *work out what you want*. What is your BHAD and how will your life be better when you achieve it? You need to positively brainstorm this. By that I mean you have to write down all the positive things that can happen if you achieve your BHAD. Any negative thoughts that come into your mind need to be quickly put aside. A positive brainstorm will paint a very attractive picture of your goal. We aren't living in dreamland. Problems and obstacles will always be present, but this is not the time to let them into the brainstorming process. Take the time to follow these few steps and see how your life changes.

- *Share your BHAD.* Telling people that you are going to run a marathon in June is a great way to commit to your goals. Publicly committing to your dream has two positives. One, you are saying your commitment aloud, thus reinforcing it. Two, it's easy to disappoint yourself with inaction, but it's much harder to disappoint others you have recruited to your dream. A training pal will make marathon training more enjoyable and spark your pride-from-inside social reward systems.

- *Start.* Sounds obvious, but as the Chinese proverb says, a journey of a thousand miles begins with a single step. My father-in-law ran twenty-four marathons. He started in his early forties and began training by doing a few laps around the local basketball courts. *Start and start now.*

- *Identify the cost of inaction.* What happens if I stay unfit? What if I stay in this job that makes me miserable? Will that make me happy? Will that improve my mood, relationships, and lifestyle? 'If you always do what you've always done, you'll always get what you've always got!'

- *Remove the barriers.* Often there are two competing priorities, and one will stop you from achieving the other. By asking yourself, 'What am I thinking, why am I thinking it, and is it helping?' you can often identify these competing issues and find a way for them to work together. Time with family and exercise may be competing priorities, but there are ways you can get the two to overlap and help everyone.

Cronk lived in the here and now. We are programmed to take more notice of the here and now. A clear vision of your BHAD will help you see that it's possible and illuminate the path to getting there. Progresstination is sneaky. Identify it and stop it now.

SELF-DECEPTION BUBBLE: WHY SMART PEOPLE DO DUMB THINGS

I have a bunch of mates that I've known for almost thirty years—intelligent, educated guys who are physically active and generally pretty health conscious. And yet, until recently, a stunningly stupid proportion of them were committed smokers. I couldn't understand it. How was it that these smart guys in their twenties and then thirties, who liked nothing better than surfing all morning, were willing to suck down expensive poison that was not only going to shorten their lives but was probably making it harder to surf? They were exposed to all the information detailing how bad smoking is. They considered themselves rational people, and yet they continued to smoke. Why do smart people do dumb things?

Cognitive dissonance is the psychological state we find ourselves in when we're faced with conflicting ideas. Be it beliefs, behaviours, or information, our brains hate contradiction and strive for internal consistency. 'I'm a smart person who smokes and all these doctors say smoking is terrible. I'm overweight and pre-diabetic, and yet I keep guzzling soft drinks and downing burgers.' These all induce cognitive dissonance that we find mentally uncomfortable, even stressful, and our brains are extremely motivated to get rid of it.

Now this sounds like a good thing. We should seek consistency in our beliefs and our perceptions. If our behaviour conflicts with our beliefs, or our beliefs conflict with some new piece of evidence or information, then we should do something about it. But there's a problem with how we deal with dissonance, and it all comes back to the Old Brain. Reducing dissonance is quick, unconscious, automatic, and takes no effort (i.e. classic Old Brain behaviour). That means it's also based on simple rules, not very nuanced, and a bit lazy. As always, the Old Brain, although great at keeping us alive, doesn't deal particularly well with the complex issues we encounter in the modern world.

When faced with information that conflicts with our beliefs or behaviours, there are a few things the New Brain can do to try and remedy the situation. Ideally, if the information is good, we should probably change our beliefs or behaviours to fit with what we now know (stop smoking). Unfortunately, this doesn't always—or even often—happen. We could also justify our beliefs or behaviours in the face of conflicting information by adding new thoughts or beliefs: everyone dies of something. I exercise more than most people. I deserve at least one vice. Or we can just ignore, deny, or downplay the information that conflicts with our belief or behaviour: who cares? Scientists say everything gives you cancer. I had an uncle who smoked and drank and lived to a hundred.

Dissonance is particularly uncomfortable when our central or core beliefs are challenged. We aren't generally bothered by a bad review of a movie we thought was good, but when it comes to things like *I'm smart but I smoke*, or *I'm an honest person but I cheated on a test*, or *I'm a good person but I failed to help someone out*, these things cause problems. It is far easier to reassess your view of the external information than reassess your opinion of yourself, so discomfort is usually resolved by devaluing and discarding a conflicting piece of knowledge or by justifying your behaviour. Even worse, the more heavily you're invested in a position, the greater lengths you will go to keep it—or justify it—which is why people who have tried to quit smoking and failed will downplay the dangers more than people who haven't even tried to quit.

Once you understand cognitive dissonance, your need to reduce, and how the Old Brain does this, you start seeing it everywhere. Ever wonder why hammering a climate sceptic with facts and figures and pointing out why all of his arguments are ridiculous never changes his mind? Instead of his thanking you for showing him the light, your suggestion that he's stupid forces his Old Brain to reduce dissonance the only way it knows how: by making him dig his heels in even further and devalue your arguments as the product of some grand conspiracy orchestrated by the UN in collaboration with the hippies.

In the 1950s some researchers[16] were thinking about initiation challenges and were wondering why people would do difficult and

---

16   Aronson and Mills, "The effect of severity of initiation on liking for a group," *Journal of Abnormal and Social Psychology* (1959), 59, p. 177–181, http://www.thinkib.net/psychology/page/7245/aronson-mills-1959.

humiliating things in order to join a club filled with people who made them do difficult and humiliating things. So they conducted an experiment. Two groups of people had to perform some task before being allowed into a discussion group that was going to talk about sex. (This was the 1950s, remember, so it was a pretty exciting prospect.)

One group had a trivial task to perform while the other had to do something a bit difficult and a bit embarrassing. The kicker was that once they had performed the entry task, instead of a salacious sex chat, they got a dry academic discussion on reproductive behaviours in animals in a group of not very nice people. So who was more annoyed about joining a lame group? Contrary to what most people expect, the group who had to do something embarrassing was less annoyed, and instead of feeling ripped off, the members commented that the discussion was actually pretty interesting and the group as a whole seemed rather nice. Rather than feel stupid, these people preferred to justify doing something embarrassing by claiming it was worth it. We make up rationalisations that make us feel less stupid.

Before making a decision like buying a car, we are at our most open to information, painstakingly researching and comparing options and alternatives. But once we make our decision and buy our car, we are mentally committed and things change drastically. From now on, we will forget about both the bad points of our car and the good points of the alternatives. Any new information we see that supports what a great decision we made will jump out at us, and anything that suggests otherwise will simply be ignored or downplayed. Our drive for post-decision justification is so immense that even bettors at a racetrack have been shown to be more confident in their chosen horse just after making a bet than before making it. Students judge cheating less harshly after they have been induced to cheat on a test, and investors throw good money after bad investments time and again when they should simply cut their losses and walk away.

So why on earth has evolution thrust such a hopeless system on us? Well, these Old Brain approaches aren't always bad, particularly in the context of a simpler world (like Cronk's). For instance, having a stable belief system is a good thing. It often does our thinking for us, making life a bit streamlined and easier, and our beliefs can help bind us to our community. This is one reason why religion has been such a big part of the human experience. Letting religion dictate what's right and wrong is easier than weighing things up for yourself. You don't want to be constantly questioning everything you believe or you'd go mad! Also, being happy with our decisions is an important coping skill. So long as things work out reasonably well most of the time, you don't want to lie awake at night obsessing whether or not you did the right thing. We need systems that make the world manageable. But like so many of our problems, it is in dealing with the complexities of the modern world that our automatic systems struggle and we have this rational New Brain sitting there just waiting to get involved. We can have the best of both worlds by letting our Old Brain do its thing—you can't stop it anyway—and then learning to use the New Brain to act as the supervisor keeping things in check and take over when it needs to.

Just knowing about cognitive dissonance is a start. Once you know about something like this, you will quickly start seeing it, and then you can do something about it, and it doesn't take much. Rather than mindlessly justifying a negative behaviour in order to protect your belief or self-esteem, you simply need to consciously rationalise why changing your behaviour and questioning your beliefs is not only okay but good. This kind of change is growth and growth is good. It's okay to be wrong sometimes, even on real core things. I can make mistakes and still be a smart, nice, kind person. In fact, I'm so together that when the facts change, I change my position and I'm grateful for it. I'm not simply losing a belief but gaining a better one that will be more useful and more helpful and make me smarter. Finally, remember dissonance when dealing with other people. If you make people feel stupid, they will not thank you for it. They will dig their heels in and resist even more your rational, logical point of view backed up with tons of evidence.

Most of the time, as with anything, we're lazy and we take the path of least resistance. Changing our actions is hard, particularly if we have an addiction like smoking. Change is the best resolution to cognitive dissonance, and yet it's the one we go to least.

Dealing with cognitive dissonance the easy way puts us in a *self-deception bubble*, which is that little place we live in when we'd rather lie to ourselves than change a particular behaviour or attitude. It's where we justify and rationalise, where 'the rules don't apply to me.' We do that all the time.

I do it all the time with food. I'm one of these people who do heaps of exercise but don't lose any weight. As the old saying goes, you can't outrun a bad diet! I love food. I love drinking beer. Chips on the table? I'm going to smash them. Some candies in the bowl? Not after I leave the room. I know I shouldn't. I know what I should eat. I know that eating is the reason why I'm not losing weight as well as I should. But I rationalize it, telling myself I'll go to the gym the next day or, because it's Friday, I'll be really good on my diet come Monday. By halfway through Tuesday, though, I'll be eating pies and mowing down burgers. I'm rationalising and justifying my bad choices in my head so I don't feel bad about them. But who am I kidding?

One of the best ways to not kid yourself anymore is to actually be aware that you're putting yourself in a bubble and to own it: 'Yeah, I'm doing this. No, I'm not going to have that, and no, I'm not going to kid myself about it. Yes, being fitter and healthier is really important to me and I'm not going to eat that packet of cookies.'

It's more of a key to willpower than just abstaining, and just being aware of what you're doing is the first step toward changing your habits. It's a bit like getting to that fork in the stress road. You've got to be aware of the point at which you go down the I'm-out-of-control road because the moment you become aware that you're in the self-deception bubble is the moment that the bubble pops.

This bubble is actually quite easy to pop with honesty and by integrating the Old and New Brains. You pop it by going back to those questions we've repeated the whole way through: What am I thinking? Why am I thinking it? Is it helping?

As soon as we start deceiving ourselves, other people have to rationalize our actions as well as their own. Eventually, they demonize one another, and that sends the culture of any relationship, personal or professional, down the toilet.

One of the things that great leaders do is avoid self-defeat. They know exactly what their good points are, and they accept their bad points. They admit their failures. They admit the things they're bad at. They allow themselves to be human, and people will follow them because of their honesty and their treating everyone else as equal. Because great leaders don't live in a self-deception bubble, they aren't so preoccupied with themselves. That allows them to go after people on their team and find out what they can do to help them, not treat them as objects that will get them where they want to go.

If you're going to be a good leader, you're going to need positive relationships with people, which means you'll need to accept their good bits and their bad bits. If people know that even their bad bits are being embraced, they'll actually do their best to improve their flaws.

But the self-deception bubble isn't just found in the workplace. Once it takes root, it becomes a part of every aspect of your life. I'll prove it to you. Let's pretend that it's 3 a.m. and you have just woken up to your baby crying. You have two choices. One is to get up and sort the baby out: feed it or change its nappy or whatever has to be done. The other is to lie there and wait for your partner to get up and do it. You have two choices: your Cronk instinct (your primal instinct) and your selfish instinct. Your primal instinct is to get up and help the baby, while your selfish instinct is to rest up for that busy day ahead of you.

The only thing that's going to stop your primal instinct is if you start justifying and rationalizing your selfish instinct: 'I have to get up early to go to work. My spouse doesn't have to go to work, so I'll get her to do it. Last time I got up and she didn't even know and she didn't even say thank you.' What you're really telling yourself is that you're more important than she is. As soon as you start saying that sort of thing, you're again putting yourself in the self-deception bubble.

We'll find these justifications and rationalizations going on in our head all the time. They stop us from doing the right thing, the primal thing, to help us contribute to our tribe. The key to popping that self-deception bubble is to be aware of yourself and catch yourself when you're making those excuses and not following what your true instincts are. That's when you're putting yourself back in a bubble in which only you matter. What would the better version of you do?

A few years ago, we had a holiday home by the beach. We tried virtually everything, but we couldn't get the grass in the backyard to grow. It was just too shady and sandy. I decided we needed a deck and proceeded to do a Google search on how to build one. My wife was genuinely scared (we've established my poor DIY record). She was convinced that I would sever a limb or build a deck that would collapse. This time it was going to be different, I thought.

It was November, and I decided to grow a moustache and raise some money for men's health. I looked like a Colombian drug dealer and everyone started to call me Carlos. I loved it. I had an alter ego, and Carlos was great! Luke is useless at DIY, but if you need a deck built, Carlos is your man. The deck took about three days to build, and when it was finished, we all sat on it, cracked a beer, and toasted to what a great job Carlos had done. Carlos is the slightly (well, significantly) better version of me.

Recently, in an attempt to link my Old and New Brains, I have been asking myself what Carlos would do. Asking my New Brain what Carlos would do is a great way to ensure my brain's supervisor is doing its job. Would Carlos be lazy and not go to the gym? *No way!* Would Carlos be brave and make the tough decision at work? *Of course he would.* Would Carlos put the washing on the line and help out around the house? *Absolutely.*

> '*Choosing to be a better version of yourself is a conscious decision to keep improving.*'
>
> **—Carlos, 2017**

The better version of yourself will not rationalise poor decisions. The better version of yourself will do the difficult task at hand and not progresstinate. The better version of yourself is authentic and thoughtful and has honest self-awareness. It's this awareness that is the final piece in the *Stress Teflon* puzzle. We aren't always the best version of ourselves, but it is really important that we always try to be.

— C O N C L U S I O N —

'Then you begin to make it better.'

— The Beatles

What does it look like when we put all the elements of this book together? A *Stress Teflon* life looks a lot like my mate Adam's experience in overcoming his own trials and tribulations. Adam Hudson is someone who is objectively flourishing. He's an entrepreneur in every sense of the word. The five companies he owns make millions of dollars and do wonderful things to improve people's lives all over the world. He has a strong tribe and helps other people to become more successful. His great contributions to others fill him with pride, but he also has a sense of honesty and self-awareness that helps him embrace his good parts as well as accept his weaknesses. *Adam has achieved eudemonia!*

Adam has a great life, but he's had to work hard for it. He has navigated the fork in the stress road before, so he knows how to take the good road when he meets the crossroads. A few years ago, however, that wasn't the case, and he found himself on a dangerous path toward self-destruction that could have taken his life.

Adam began his adult life in Browns Plains, a working-class, outer suburb of Brisbane. His first job earned him $183 a week, working in a one-hour photo shop before he took a job as a door-to-door salesman with Kirby vacuum cleaners. That was his first exposure to sales and the world of personal development books and speakers. That's where things started to change after his managers told him to listen to Zig Ziglar and Jim Rohn motivational tapes and read Anthony Robbins's books.

His first successful business was selling personal development courses for an American company. He started part-time, keeping his full-time job. By the age of twenty-three, he left his full-time job and focused on his new sales company, which eventually had hundreds of distributors working for him around Australia. He sold that company at the age of twenty-five and since then he has owned seventeen different companies, including a hair salon in Sydney, a flight simulator in Los Angeles, a finance company that went public on the stock exchange, and an animation studio in Hollywood that he sold in 2015. He now also has a large business helping other people sell products on Amazon.

Everything changed a few years ago when Adam walked out of his office in Los Angeles and started to feel a bit dizzy and weak in the knees. 'I'm not feeling too good', he said to his colleague. The next thing he knew he was waking up in an ambulance on the way to hospital. A barrage of tests concluded that, physically, he was fine, but a severe panic attack had simply shut down his body, causing him to pass out without warning. No way! He was Superman, a man bulletproof to stress, or so he thought. His body had decided otherwise.

As we talked about in chapter 5, Adam's body turned off the things that weren't essential, and in his case, that meant virtually everything. It was a kind of rebooting issued by his brain, and it gave Adam the kick up the arse he needed. He went to Bali and spent two months surfing, doing yoga, and learning to meditate. He learnt how to link his Old and New Brains and discovered the self-awareness needed to juggle all the balls he had in the air. He unpacked his life and realised why he was exhausted.

The penny-drop moment for Adam was when he was asked to tell about a time he experienced pure joy. He took three or four minutes to think of one. It took a while longer for him to make a list of things in his life that brought him joy and a list of the things he did in his day-to-day life. When he looked at the two lists, there was almost no overlap. Things had to change. Making lists, asking hard questions, and having a good, hard look at ourselves in a room of mirrors, so to speak, creates the mind awareness we need to connect our two brains.

By connecting to gratitude and answering the three most important questions when dealing with stress—What am I thinking? Why am I thinking it? And is it helping?—Adam managed to find more joy in his life while still pursuing the goals that gave him his *pride from inside*.

Just how far Adam had come became apparent recently when Amazon announced a change in policy that rendered one of his companies obsolete—overnight. His business I Love to Review was a highly profitable, multimillion-dollar company that provided reviews of products on Amazon. By changing the rules regarding reviews, Amazon made Adam's company and its staff and contributors redundant, costing him a fortune in lost revenue. That is *really* stressful. Adam had other companies, and financially, he was still safe, but a blow like that could easily cripple a person mentally and cause another stress overload. It didn't! Adam was disappointed—his situation was less than ideal, he thought—but his newly developed awareness gave him the skills to ride this out. The stress just didn't stick.

His main concern was not for himself but for the staff he employed at I Love to Review. 'They are all talented and we will help get them other jobs', he explained. 'They are all just sad they won't get to come to work at such a great place.' Adam had developed a culture that made his people feel safe and appreciated. They were part of his tribe. This is what the staff and Adam were going to miss.

Adam has the fast cars, the big house, and the great boat. These things are toys and by-products of being successful. They are not the reason he does what he does. They aren't Adam's BHAD, which is to develop a community where people are safe and thrive together, a tribe where people help each other to *do* things that give them *pride from inside*, a place where *tend and befriend* is more important than *fight or flight*. And today Adam is healthy and thriving, both in business and in spirit. He connects his mind and body with yoga and mind awareness, which has helped him stay mindful of how he ticks: what to seek out in his life and work and what to avoid. He may have lots of stress in his life, but it doesn't stick, doesn't weigh him down and chip away at his health, wealth, and spirit. And that's what being *Stress Teflon* is all about.

You don't need to be an international entrepreneur or have multiple businesses to become *Stress Teflon*, either. Take Bill, for example. At fifty-five years old, Bill is unemployed, has no family, and lives in government housing. He struggles to put up with people's bullshit, as he calls it, and that makes keeping a job really difficult. Surviving on unemployment benefits, he doesn't have much money or a flashy car, but he is *Stress Teflon*.

Bill is a busy man, too. He works in a soup kitchen every morning and cooks sausages at the local hardware store to make money for the soup kitchen. He spends three nights a week volunteering at the local merry-go-round, helping kids onto it and taking their $1 donation that raises money for the local Rotary Club.

Bill has a tribe, he has great self-awareness, and he contributes. His days are dedicated to helping others. He may not be pretty or rich, and he definitely doesn't get the political correctness of modern society, but Bill loves being Bill. Choosing to be happy, practicing mind awareness, and contributing to your tribe all cost nothing, but they all add to your positivity and help you put the stressors of a modern world into perspective.

Understanding fear, connecting your Old and New Brains, and understanding where your stress originates are the keys to putting things into perspective. Catching yourself what-iffing and developing self-awareness will ensure you go down the positive stress road. By striving to be the better version of yourself and contributing to your tribe, you get your *pride from inside*.

So I say again that stress is not the enemy! Embrace the good stress and let the toxic stress slide off. Once you do, you will find the objective flourishing of *eudemonia* and become *Stress Teflon*. And no matter who you are, it's good being you when you're *Stress Teflon*.

Printed in the USA
CPSIA information can be obtained
at www.ICGtesting.com
JSHW011658200524
63486JS00014B/96/J